HR, Where's Your Freaking Sense of Humor?

Carol McBride, PHR, SHRM-CP

HR, WHERE'S YOUR FREAKING SENSE OF HUMOR?

Carol McBride

Published by: The Carol McBride Group, LLC

Published in the United States of America

ISBN-13:978-0692604960
ISBN-10:0692604960 (Amazon)

Dedication

Affectionately dedicated to the man of my dreams, Bobby,
and my supercalifragilisticexpialidocious daughter and son,
Ashley and Jonathon. Thank you for being my biggest fans
and supporting me on this journey! Merrily, merrily,
merrily, merrily, life is but a dream ...with you by my side.

A Special Thank You From the Author

To EVERYONE who believed in my dreams and laughed and cried (just a little) with me on this journey. Thank you all for your financial, spiritual, and mental support, as it was sincerely appreciated. Thank you for your prayers and words of encouragement along the way. Special thanks to my mom for being my prayer warrior, to my "Innermost Circle" for answering my call to action, even when life was hectic for you, and to my talented and creative illustrator, Suzanne Powell, for transforming my thoughts into amazing artwork. Please believe that your names will be forever engraved in my heart.

Contents

Preface

It's a wonder that human resources professionals don't run out of the office every day screaming the chorus to Marvin Gaye's acclaimed hit "Mercy, Mercy Me." Dealing with negative coworkers, management failures, involuntary terminations, conflict resolutions, bad bosses, and surprise mergers and acquisitions are among the top ten human resources issues that HR professionals deal with on a daily basis.

Hence, my inspiration for the first in a series of books about HR follies based on my personal experiences during my 20-year HR career. I also draw inspiration from my HR mentors, colleagues, and friends on days when HR issues and situations are complex, mindboggling, heartrending, and downright treacherous. When asked how I navigate through the unique but trying situations and challenges, I simply state, "With a respectful sense of humor, of course."

My goal and hopes for readers is that they will laugh when at times the situation may make them feel like crying or giving up and throwing in the white HR towel. I want to encourage HR generalists, specialists, business partners, analysts, directors, and vice presidents to stay in the ring but to remember to return to their corners (better known as their HR colleagues, chapters, associations, or self-help groups) for words of encouragement. You see, HR professionals are among the most-cut women and men in the business, and they will have plenty of Vaseline and Band-Aids to mend the proverbial cuts to our colleagues heart and confidence. Once the wounded are on the mend, they will passionately advise their HR colleagues to get back in the ring and keep fighting for their internal customers (i.e., employees) who depend on them to fight all twelve rounds every day.

The following is Carol's challenge to readers:

- To use the phrases "sense of humor" and "human resources" in the same sentence.

- Dismiss the HR myth that human resources people do not have a sense of humor.

- Prove that phrase "sense of humor" and "human resources" is an "awfully good" oxymoron.

Connect Online:

Visit my website: www.carolmcbridegroup.com

Become Facebook Friends: Carol McBride Group

Follow me on Twitter: caroldidthat

See me on Instagram: Carol.McBride

Connect on LinkedIn: Carol-McBride-PHR-SHRM-CP

Book or email me: admin@carolmcbridegroup.com

Introduction

Can you honestly say the words "sense of humor" and "human resources" in the same sentence? Should it come as a surprise that human resources professionals DO have a sense of humor? The most common HR misconception and stereotype is that HR professionals do *not* have a sense of humor. But this is quite to the Mary, Mary, quite contrary! Truth be told, a sense of humor is an undocumented prerequisite to an HR job description. Even if it is not listed in the job description under the bullet "people person with great interpersonal skills," an HR professional must read between the blurred lines. The old adage "laugh to keep from crying" is the calling card or mantra of HR professionals near and far after a not-so-typical day of HR follies. Standup comedy and *America's Funniest Videos* will find it hard to compete with a day in the life of an HR professional.

HR professionals, near and far, can tell you that a day in the life of an HR generalist can quickly change from a typical to a not-so-typical day in an instant-oatmeal-time-zone minute. Add a dash of conflict resolution (revolution), confidentiality (off the record), surprise mergers and acquisitions, creative accusations of favoritism, bad bosses and managers, rumors of inappropriate use of hands (not NFL style), and subjective (not objective) performance reviews and you have all the makings of a true comedy.

So take a moment to laugh at just a few of my HR follies and experiences because I wholeheartedly believe that laughter is the best medicine. I call having a sense of humor a stress buster for the issues that HR professionals deal with 24 hours a day, 7 days a week, 365 days a year (no off days!). I unequivocally believe it's time for the old HR stereotypes to be handed their at-will employer letter of termination. In HR, *we do people* (no inappropriate touching, of course) and *we are in the people business*, period. We are equipped with keen interpersonal skills, a high level of empathy, and the best darn gut-feeling Geiger counters money can buy. In the end, we are careful to represent all those who trust us because, in the words of some of the best comedians, "timing is everything."

Each chapter is filled with moments that I believe all HR professionals, despite their tenure, can relate to and draw inspiration from or simply look back (or forward) and know that they are not alone on this emotional HR roller coaster. I want HR professionals near and far (and even farther) to know that it's perfectly acceptable to have a sense of humor, even when dealing with some of the most serious HR dilemmas and drama kings and queens. Included in each chapter are also industry statistics, quotes from subject-matter experts, and best HR practices and reminders. As an added bonus, I include hilarious cartoon illustrations that depict situations highlighted in the chapter to further invoke laughter and capture my unique sense of humor.

You will also discover:

- It is absolutely acceptable to have a sense of humor in HR.

- HR has evolved and come a long way, baby!

- There is no such thing as a typical day in HR—so keeping hands, arms, and legs inside the ride at all times for safety purposes while on this HR roller coaster is required.

- Demanding a seat at the decision-making table is not optional, it's required—so don't forget the dinner napkin for notes.

- Every HR professional needs at least one HR mantra to combat the chance of waving the white flag when the next BIG company initiative is announced.

- HR professionals are known for being motivation fire starters—so knowing the location of the nearest fire extinguisher is crucial because once they motivate employees to be the "best they can be," the fire they ignite may not be extinguishable by water alone.

- Simple employee policy revisions and precautionary best practices may keep your ass(ets) out of court and help you avoid threats by employees to sue the company.

Notes to the Reader

- The word "freaking" is used throughout the book to emphasize humor and the title.

- The Moments of Truth throughout the book contain true-life examples from my HR career.

- The Fast-Forward moments are transitions from Moments of Truth back to the present.

- The Pause Moments are breaks from the story line to further expand on a thought related to the topic.

- My own HR mantra is included at the end of each chapter.

So before you turn the page, I want you to remember the old adage, "Laughter is the best medicine" ... not "An apple a day" because you remember what happened to Eve and Snow White.

Laugh on, my dear friends!!!

1

HR Mantra

Mantra: noun man·tra \ 'män-trə also 'man- or 'mən-\: a word or phrase that is repeated often or that expresses someone's basic beliefs[1]

Day after day, you serve in your respective HR role and steadily build a foundation of what you believe a true HR professional looks like. You apply your knowledge, skills, and abilities (KSA) with fortitude and dignity. You uphold the code of ethics and conduct of the company and strongly encourage others to do the same. You attend Society for Human Resource Management (SHRM) conferences and seminars on a regular basis so you may surround yourself with others who do the same. Your goal while in that forum is to increase your acumen and knowledge in the area of human resources management and all it embodies. You then return to the office and reenact, implement, and translate all you have learned into laymens terms and identify opportunities for application and applicability.

In your daily interactions with skilled, administrative, and managerial employees, your goal is to convey an atmosphere of fairness, hope, and empathy. Conveying these positive attributes takes a creative HR professional who is willing to inspire others through his or her written or spoken words. Keep calm; this is not a challenge for you to take the Comedy Central stage and belt out a rhythmic improvisation of your not-so-typical day in HR. This is an official challenge to you to create and define your own HR mantra and to convey and communicate it to others as part of your daily routine. For instance, your inspiration for your first of many HR mantras can be drawn from your Oscar award-winning triumphs over adversity or your "wake me when it's over" failures. It's your choice. Once you have chosen your systematic approach, my edict to you is to believe in it, speak it, and make it part of your rules to live by. Here are a few memorable mantras to kick-start your creativity:

- "I decided to stick with love. Hate is too great a burden." Dr. Martin Luther King, Jr.

- "Be the change you wish to see in the world." Gandhi

- "Only do what your heart tells you." Princess Diana

- "Just do it." Nike

- "Fears are stupid, so are regrets." Marilyn Monroe

- "Start where you are. Do what you can. Use what you can." Arthur Ashe

These are only a few of the powerful mantras from ordinary people who went on to do and achieve extraordinary things. It is even said that mantras are medicine for the soul and help ease the mind. Just this lineup of mantras alone confirms that every HR professional needs a mantra because you will, or have already, heard and witnessed incidents that would make most people cringe, cry, or run for the hills while waving their resignation letter in surrender.

Okay, okay. Let's put down our white flags because one thing we know for certain is that HR professionals are not quitters. This was just a brief moment of freaking panic, and you are all better now. The truth of the matter is that sometimes you just need an HR mantra to help you get through the day, the week, the quarter—or through the freaking year! Your mantra could be something as simple as the following:

- "It is what it is."

- "I'll never do *that* again."

- "Better luck next time."

- "You win some, and you lose some."

- "Am I being punked?"

- "I will live to fight another day."

- "Run away and don't look back!"

I think you get where I'm coming from. Some HR mantras are temporary and meant to encourage yourself so you can make it through a not-so-typical day in HR (Chapter 8). So whether you want to be inspired on a day when life seems to have you on the ropes, or you want to inspire others to live to fight another day, or you think it's time to throw in the towel and let someone else take over, remember that your HR mantra will be there waiting to lead you home ... to that glass of wine, or out of the darkness into the light—or to the freaking safe word: "pineapple!".

Now is the time you pick up a blank piece of paper, envelope or smartphone and bang out your HR mantra. Don't delay ... take the next steps to create and develop your mantra that will inspire and light a fire in your heart and in the minds of others you will touch (not literally touch, as that will quickly change your HR mantra to a lawsuit). And if all else fails, go to Successories.com and order those wonderful framed posters for your office to unleash your creative side that may have become stifled by the rigor of your not-so-typical days in HR.

While it may be challenging at first, I guarantee that you will get the hang of it and will be banging out mantras like a world-class motivator in no time.

Believe what you say
because words live on long after the sunset.

2

HR Mentors, Where Would You Be?

Where would I be without my HR mentor? This is a question for the general HR community and one you may ask at some point in your career.

Flashbacks of the first time you expressed interest in an HR role may be vivid or have faded a bit, but they are good memories nevertheless. And memories of your one or multiple mentors may also come to mind. You remember the mentor who shared with you that you are a people person and that the HR community needs you. It sounded like a call from Uncle Sam to join the military, but you didn't panic because you knew the draft was over in 1973. You remember choosing your role based on the fantastic overview from your mentor on the different facets of HR. And it was your mentor's encouragement and reassurance that gave you the courage to take on your first HR role as a generalist, recruiter, analyst, specialist, business partner, director, vice president, or (you fill in the blank).

If you haven't realized it yet or grown into your HR shoes, HR professionals are the best storytellers this side of Planet Hollywood. We are right up there with the real estate agents who sell swampland in Louisiana. We have been said to be the dream employees of the VPs of sales and marketing—until they find out that we hate to be forced to meet a sales quota of any kind.

Now back to your decision to join the HR ranks and how the gentle nudge or firm push of your mentor put you on the road to HR bliss. Okay, too much? How about HR nirvana? Still too much? How about a satisfying career in HR? No matter how you were led, I hope the day, week, or month is memorable and the story is one you will tell those you will mentor later in your career.

You also recall the admirable traits and observations you made about your mentor, which reaffirmed how fortunate you were to have forged this lasting relationship, such as:

- the pride and confidence your mentor possessed day after day,

- the respect given to him or her by peers during strategic and tough conversations, and

- how during meetings, people hung on his or her every word, and responses were held until your mentor had expressed his or her opinion.

You probably have thought to yourself, Is this person real? And when does he or she duck into a phone booth to don a superhero outfit and cape? (You've got to have a cape to be cool!) The reality is that these people do exist and are considered our heroes—even without the cape. To have a mentor means someone genuinely cares about you, your career, and your well-being. The crowning moments are when you are granted opportunities to shadow your mentor during meetings and accompany him or her on business trips.

Moment of Truth: I have been blessed to mentor several professionals in my career. A few have been through official mentoring programs, but many others have simply requested my guidance and mentorship. Despite the introduction, I was honored and humbled with every request and took the opportunity very seriously. I believe that when you are asked to pour knowledge into mentees, the fluid must be pure and pasteurized, for their empty vessels should never be filled with tainted goods. Even as I embarked on this journey to write my first book, I received notes of appreciation from former mentees sharing how much they have grown because of my willingness to teach and empower them.

Pause Moment: Mentoring in the workplace has not always been a bona fide program in which the company matched a high-potential employee with a mentor. Nor has it always been an official directive from on high with the clearly defined objective of helping employees develop new skills and engaging them with the company. Rather, it was those great mentors within the company who believed that mentoring was the right thing to do. They reached deep within their cluttered schedules, without the guidelines of a program or threats of reduced bonuses, and organically mentored their employees to become future leaders.

The good news is that mentoring in general has always been a part of the fabric of our lives (like cotton), and many have been the benefactors of this act of kindness. The following are a few quotations from some people you may know who emphasize the importance of mentoring[2]:

- "Tell me and I forget, teach me and I may remember, involve me and I learn." Benjamin Franklin

- "I am not a teacher, but an awakener." Robert Frost

- "Inspiration is a tool and a trap. If you're going to be inspired by anyone, be inspired by people who have been exactly where you are now." Douglas Copeland

- "It's hard to renounce heroes unless you have one to start with." Joseph Bottum

- "We were motivated by our mentors to go an extra mile." Lailah Gifty Akita[3]

- "Your most important task as a leader is to teach people how to think and ask the right questions so that the world doesn't go to hell if you take a day off." Jeffrey Pfeffer

As you read each quote, I hope you were able to relate to a single word if not the entire statement and that you experienced these qualities firsthand under the responsible guidance of your mentor. Even one of the most famous inventors in the history of the world, Benjamin Franklin, understood that teaching and involving an employee in the learning process reaps the greatest dividends. I wonder if it was he who left the details for the new long-lasting battery with his mentee? Probably not. But if we fast-forward to today, his invention is the driving force behind the latest technology, and new variations of batteries are on the horizon because he decided to pass on his knowledge. I think you get the Mona Lisa I am trying to paint. And how about that riveting statement by Sir Robert Frost? If I was asleep before, I am AWAKE now! That statement just makes me want to go out and find more mentees *today*!

HR professionals know that mentoring has gained traction and is now formally recognized by companies. Our role is to keep these programs alive and encourage participation. HR's role is also to remain innovative and not allow these programs to stall or become underutilized. For instance, the latest in innovative mentoring practices is called reverse mentoring. Contrary to the traditional mentoring model, reverse mentoring pairs a member of upper management with a younger employee in the company. In this model, the younger employee is the mentor and the senior manager is the mentee. Did you know that reverse mentoring was actually championed by Jack Welch when he was chief executive of General Electric? So while not new, it is innovative and can breathe life back into a tired mentoring program.

According to *The Wall Street Journal*, Mr. Welch ordered five hundred top-level executives to reach out to people below them to learn how to use the Internet.[4] Mr. Welch himself was matched with an employee in her twenties who taught him how to surf the Web. This model is a win-win proposition because the young mentor gains visibility and the mentee manager learns how to use technology and gains knowledge of social media and workplace-trends.

Need a few more mentoring program benefits? The *Houston Chronicle* shared the following[5]:

- employers gain from greater productivity in workplace (e.g., fewer mistakes),

- increases employee job satisfaction,

- reduces employee turnover and increases worker loyalty, and

- attracts new employees to company.

Fast-Forward to your HR mentor relationship and what comes next. This is always the greatest part of the story because you are now responsible for taking what has been instilled and invested in you and applying it to your real-life experiences and career. The seed has been sown, and the next step is to grow and flourish. The key is to responsibly use this gift and, most importantly, share it with others when the time is right.

   As I conclude this chapter, there is one task I would encourage you to complete today. Send a note of thanks to your mentor (or mentors), thanking him or her for investing in you and relaying that your stock value has continued to exceed projected returns.

   Knowledge is meant to be given away, not kept.

3

HR, Evolution or Revolution?

Let's face it, "old grey mule, you ain't what [you] used to be."[6] Simply stated, the HR of old has come and gone, and the scope, breadth, and depth have changed—domestically and internationally. The days of administration and files filled with applications, personnel change notices, write-ups, pink slips, and handbook acknowledgment forms have passed through the tunnel of love and emerged with the facelift affectionately referred to as workforce, human capital, human resource information system (HRIS), employment law, performance management, succession planning, strategy with a large dose of change management, and a dash of the ever-vigilant team building.

HR evolution can be likened to the generations of life. From birth to the time a person's career begins and retirement is imminent, time passes, and the circumstances of life are etched in our history, and the new society simplifies who we are by slapping a generational label on our foreheads. As such, HR professionals near and far have been forced to incorporate this age-based description into our day-to-day nomenclature when trying to identify with employee behaviors, competencies, and succession and workforce-planning initiatives.

Let us begin with the Traditionalist and Silent Generations, who are subgenerations of the Greatest Generation. Traditionalists and Silents were born between 1901 and 1945. Traditionalists are described as hard workers and are known for their commitment to civic duty and military service. Silents are described as children of World War I heroes who were too young to join the service. It is from these generations that traditionalist HR gurus were born. Notice there is no reference to silent HR gurus; this is because they were also described as morally confused and fatalistic. Hence their silence.

During this period, HR structured its policies and procedures around the characteristics of the Traditionalist beliefs and the industrial era. The defining moment in an HR professional's life during this era was to be referred to by the workforce as the personnel department. The primary role of the personnel department was to serve people. But what did that mean? Well, it meant that as long as a person was sitting at his or her desk managing the large volume of paperwork and hiring demands of the company, life in the personnel department was good and management credited the personnel department for a job well done. Success was measured by how many file cabinets one could fill with paper because the record retention policy had not yet been born. The personnel files were likely to have employee paperwork dating back to the early eighteenth century.

This was a time of uncertainty for many people. Men had responded to the draft in America and were called to arms to protect the country. But let us not forget that it was not just men who were called to serve; women were also called to serve in health-care roles to aid and care for the wounded discharged from the rigors of war. Although many women served, many stayed behind to hold down the fort they called home. But both women and men during this era became the new clients or customers of the personnel department. They completed applications, shared their skills and experiences, and were advised by the personnel department on their pay and benefits and workplace policies. The conversations were generally one-sided, and the expectations were simple: you work, and we pay you.

But let's not be too pretentious or sarcastic because in reality some of the best, most evolutionary practices are a result of the Traditionalist personnel regimen. If it wasn't for the high volume of paper and transactions that were manually processed by these great professionals, we would never have been able to coin the phrase "going paperless" and invent the tools that catapulted us into the world of electronic filing systems. You see, the evolution of HR has always been a result of examining a practice and then brainstorming how we can do it better, faster, and more efficiently.

Emerging next were the Baby Boomers, the children of the Traditionalist and the Silent Generations (who we later determined weren't very traditional or silent since they gave birth to over 77 million babies over a span of 42 years!). This generation made up over 40 percent of the United States population by 1964. And if ever a HR strategy on workforce planning was needed, it was after 1968 when the first Boomers became 18 years of age.

The workforce predominately consisted of soldiers returning home after serving in World War II, the Korean War, and the Vietnam War. According to CNN's article "Baby Boomer Generation Fast Facts," the average age of a solider during this time was 19 years old and the household demographics were likely to consist of a wife and 2.3 children.[7] How in the freaking Einstein theory of relativity did Americans come up with a decimal point in the tenth numerical position to describe a family size? I will leave that to the accountants since I am strictly HR. However, turn the clock forward to 2014 and the long line of parents who wish they were only responsible for 2.3 of each of their children's financial needs. But then they hear on a breaking news report that the Affordable Care Act, affectionately known as Obamacare, has been passed. Financial reality sets in because now their son or daughter living in the basement can remain on their medical insurance until age 26 and never leave home!

Amongst a few of the most popular jobs during this era were skilled manufacturers, nurses, lawyers, realtors, appraisers, and farmers. By 2011, more than 25 percent of the workforce was scheduled to retire from the manufacturing industry. An article titled "Baby Boomers" says that so many babies were born during this era that you could hear the cries across the country.[8] But I bet the cries of HR professionals across America were probably louder when they realized that a succession plan for these retirees was not in place!

Simple math recap: If there are 77 million Boomers and only 40 million Generation Xers, who will backfill the roughly 37 million jobs when they retire? Houston, we have a problem! It was also during this era that personnel departments across America experienced what it felt like to be responsible for hiring thousands of blue-collar workers to fill the open positions. Type "a typical day in the life of a blue-collar assembly-line worker at Ford Motor Company" in your favorite Web browser for an eye-opening perspective. The video clip will also provide a bird's-eye view of the sheer number of people it took to assemble a single vehicle. The best visual by far comes from a video clip of the 1979 movie *Norma Rae*.

Moment of Truth: Quite frankly, I personally did not have to search too far for an example of how blue-collar workers viewed life and the personnel department, because my mother was "all about that assembly-line life" for as long as I can remember. She and her colleagues frequently spoke about the long hours on the assembly line making telephone pieces over and over and over again until the chief inspector placed her initials on the finished product. She spoke of the infamous pay grades that were always followed by the Roman numerals I, II, III, IV, and V (if you were lucky). However, she spoke very little about the presence of the personnel department, unless someone was scheduled to retire after thirty years of service or a dreaded factory shutdown or layoff was imminent.

The good news about Generation X is that they are described as independent, hardworking, and mature beyond their years because they had Traditionalist and Baby Boomer parents who walked ten miles every day, uphill both ways to school in a snowstorm in the South (I hope you caught the inconsistencies in this story, as I am sure you have heard many over the years). According to human resources expert Susan Heathfield, "They [Baby Boomers] want to build a repertoire of skills and experiences they can take with them if they need to, and they want their career path laid out in front of them—or they'll walk."[9] So to keep their boots from walking, 'cause that's just what they'll do, HR had to step in … to keep them boots from walking all over you … I mean, walk all over the company. (If you didn't catch it, this was my best Patsy Cline impression.)

Fast-Forward: As of 2012, Boomers make up 24 percent of the total US population, approximately 315,000,000! More simple math: There are 77 million Baby Boomers but only 46 million in the generation after them, the Generation X population. So even if 100 percent of the Generation Xers move into the positions held by the hardworking Baby Boomers, this will still leave a surplus of approximately 30 million jobs for the taking. Hence, the HR birth announcement reads, "Traditionalist and Baby Boomer personnel department just gave birth to a ten-pound Generation X HR department with the assistance of an epidural, and the anesthesiologist wasn't covered by insurance!"

During this era, HR is now the first line of defense, or offense, depending on the internal customer who decides to visit its office on any given day. If the customer is a manager coming to share that a high-performing Generation Xer just gave him an ultimatum to increase her pay or she will walk (or run) to the competitor who, she stated, was paying a dollar more an hour and giving three fifteen-minute breaks a day, then it is defense time. If it is the employee who strongly believes that he is being treated unfairly because he is amongst the minority in the department, then it is offense time and HR has to put in its best players to swiftly remedy the situation.

Right before the eyes of the world and God, HR has organically transformed into the "people people" we have grown to love today because of our need to engage with the workforce to build and repair relationships. HR has been called to a tour of duty in desert storm corners of the west wing of the building, thereby allowing the company to focus on the core business (at least that is what we read in the board meeting minutes). Less and less time can be devoted to paperwork and more and more time to workforce planning, training and development, and succession planning. Lest we forget the simple math mentioned earlier, and the 30 million open positions that have to be posted on Monster.com by the end of the decade. I believe a great big "thank you" to Generation X is in order for making us change our thinking and embrace change management strategies (figuratively embrace, not literally, so as to avoid a sexual harassment claim).

So just when you thought the party was almost over, and the water that Jesus turned into wine was about to run out, again, in come the Millennials, shouting, "The party ain't over yet!" in their best eighties hip-hop voice. HR professionals had a momentary brain freeze when this generation arrived on the scene at 9:30-ish Monday morning still wearing the clothes from the college football game from the night before.

This generation should have been named the "Sleeper Generation," as management and HR both may have overslept and underestimated how different they were from any of the prior generations. This missed phenomenon may have perhaps been laced with a bit of complacency since those Generation Xers had finally settled in and were pleased with the efforts and response of the HR community. Call it what you may, the Millennial Generation came in with a long grocery list of expectations and had their mother's and father's telephone numbers on speed dial in their smartphone if their demands were not met. Subsequently, while they were not quite familiar with what their demands were, they wanted to have their cake and eat it too and had no problem with working less than two weeks and moving on to bigger and better things without hesitation since they were on their parents' medical insurance plan anyway. While they did not understand who the Internal Revenue Service (IRS) was, what was the Federal Insurance Contribution Act (FICA) and Federal Unemployment Tax Act (FUTA), or how to complete a W-4, they knew how to make a computer do wonderful and magnificent things, as well as manage the heck out of a special project.

The White House Council of Economic Advisers published a report in 2014 sharing distinct facts about Millennials, including that they are 1) the largest, most diverse generation in the United States and make up one-third of the population, 2) more connected to technology than previous generations because they are the first generation to have had access to the Internet during their formative years, and 3) contrary to popular perceptions, actually are staying with their employers longer than Generation Xers did at the same ages.[10] So in laymen's terms, 1) the Millennials have a bigger team, dude, 2) they were born with a remote control in their hands so they can program anything, and 3) HR professionals, it is time to get creative, get smarter, and get ready because Millennials are here to stay.

So just as HR professionals manage to grasp the intricacy of the generational evolution, the revolution of workplace change appeared on the scene, pleading for attention. You see, evolution is a dirty job but somebody's got to do it, and more times than not, a revolution occurs shortly after an evolution has been announced. For example, think back when companies announced that employees would now be required to enter a self-service, Web-based portal and enter their hours, vacation, and benefit election *online*. The evolution definitely sparked a revolution amongst employees, as many exclaimed that they were not technologically savvy and that this was HR's job, not theirs! We savvy and sophisticated HR professionals coined it "enabling technologies and social-collaboration tools to promote innovation and sustainability." Boy, did that sound great rolling off the tongue!

But all jokes aside, HR is equally responsible for identify strategies that will accommodate the changing nature of the workforce. Hence the scheduling of targeted employee communication campaigns and lunch-and-learns to 1) respond to the revolutionary behavior and 2) explain the logic of the evolution to the online self-service concept. (Gentle Reminder: serve lunch to get them into the room.)

Then there's the revolution that occurred when the company and HR announced the transition from personal office spaces to cubicles and the open-area concept. Someone pull the fire alarm because that evolutionary move sparked a bonfire that could be seen in outer space. Thoughts of nonunion employees with picket signs outside the HR department were close to becoming a reality. The chatter, I mean shouts, exclaiming, "Whose bright idea was this?" could be heard around the hemisphere. According to Glassdoor and *Scientific American* (2009), it was the bright ideas of architects and designers "who were trying to make the world a better place—who thought that to break down the social walls that divide people, you had to break down the real walls, too."[11]

Somebody break out the 1960s peace and love memorabilia because this change actually sparked the opposite. Hence another HR reactive-based communication campaign outlining the pros (less the cons) of the transition. Below is a list of a few of the pros, laced with a sense of humor, of course, for your reading pleasure.

Pros	Translation
Improved relations with colleagues	Think of it this way: now you don't have to eavesdrop using a cup to the wall anymore.
Increased knowledge through cross-pollination	Receive instant validation that you are the smartest one in the bunch.
Exposure may lead to greater productivity	Place order for a screen protector tomorrow so they can't see your fantasy football picks.
Room for personal expression	Break out the picture of your kids, spouse, pets, or family vacations for all the world to see!

It is important to note that this change to the workspace environment is still the topic of HR and logistic discussions everywhere. Most employees have decided to lay down their arms and just go with the flow if it means they can still collect a paycheck. Score: Revolution 1, Evolution 10!

Yes, the list of changes in the workplace that often trigger revolutions is long, but the good news is that with the help of marketing, communication, managers, and senior management, HR has been able to navigate through the smoke of the musket gunpowder and proudly score win after win for evolution.

Life is evolution, so live it.

4

HR, Seat at the Table ... No, Not the Dinner Table!

Have you ever been asked, "Who are the decision makers in this company?" Did you immediately respond, "HR," or did you pause and then respond with a politically correct, "Our C-suite"? Well, welcome to the club if your answer was the latter because at some point in your career, you realized HR is not always a part of the decision-making team at your company. Yes, this means that most often HR didn't securing a seat at the table, and no, I don't mean the dinner table.

You may recall the numerous times you received an e-mail, memorandum, or telephone call with a new directive from the upper echelon of the company. Your mission (if you decided to accept it) was to rollout, communicate, or implement the new directive without a minute to think or spare, even when it had "Mission Impossible" written all over it. Time and time again, your response was "How can I help?" or "I'll get right on it" or "I'll schedule a meeting to begin the brainstorming session." At that moment, you envisioned a picture of yourself in the dictionary next to the phrase "Yes Man" or "Yes Woman" and kicked yourself after you hung up the phone, saying, "What is the freaking matter with me? Have I gone brain dead? This is freaking impossible!"

You were even a bit irritated that the words "change management" were not even mentioned by the C-suite and that the deadline would not allow you and your team to effectively manage this new directive. At that moment, your ears started burning and your heart pounding and you exclaimed, "Why wasn't HR at the table during the initial and final decision-making process?!"

Just to be clear, you did not really need an answer to this question; you just had to say what other HR professionals on your team were thinking but were too afraid or hesitant to say to the almighty management team. You lost your marbles because you couldn't help but think back to the numerous failed initiatives when HR was invited to the table too late and vividly remember how employees responded to the "news." The best words to describe their responses included but were not limited to:

- Surprised

- Angered

- Confused and dazed

- Disengaged

- Disappointed

- A few other *censored* words (use your imagination)

You also remembered all the telephone calls from employees asking, "Does this mean my job is in jeopardy?" or "Will my job change in any way?" You recalled the feeling in the pit of your stomach when the honest answer was yes, but you were not at liberty to say so at that time. It was your duty to give a creative HR response even though you knew the company was delaying the inevitable.

Just these memories alone are enough to give you heart palpitations and raise your blood pressure. So you decide that today is the day that you have a serious discussion with your boss and explain the importance of having HR at the table during the pre-decision-making stage. But prior to that meeting (after you have calmed your nerves using the conflict-management skills you were taught in the seminar last year), you will outline the business case for inclusion in the decision-making process, hoping to paint the picture why having HR at the table is GOOD and exclusion is ALL BAD. Your list will be short and concise but firm enough so your point is 0.5mm (i.e., soft but precise):

- Manage fear.

- Defuse rumor mill.

- Reduce stress (never truly eliminate).

- Manage expectations.

- Give you enough time to ensure that your offer letters and employee handbook actually have the "at will" employment clause and that active employees actually did sign the handbook receipt (just kidding—actually, I am *not* kidding!).

In all seriousness, the goal is to confidently outline HR change-management-objectives that will secure a permanent seat at the table. Oops, did I say permanent? I believe this word was to be struck from the ancient HR offer letter hieroglyphics over fifteen years ago.

You will also remind the executives on how the inclusion of the HR team will aid in setting realistic policies and developing sound change-management strategies rather than being viewed as the HR police, employee relations central, and policy hall monitors. Your agenda will be to prove that senior HR professionals talk the same language as the C-suite, finance, operations, sales and marketing, and information technology executives.

Before the meeting with your boss, you pause and say to yourself, "Do they think HR speaks another language and that is the real reason for excluding us from the decision-making process?" But you quickly talk yourself off the ledge and exclaim, also to yourself, "Absolutely not. That's freaking ridiculous! So get in there and show them what you are made of!"

*"Our employees are important."

At the end of your discussion, you are hopeful that it is crystal clear that HR:

1. speaks the same language;

2. can be decisive, methodical, and analytical;

3. can assess complex situations and bring new ideas and options to the table;

4. views a key performance indicator (KPI) as a viable component of doing business;

5. can and will set policies and practices that allow the company to recruit and retain a qualified workforce;

6. can be strategic too (whoever said we can't, needs to face the music and name that tune in one note!); and

7. is the monitor of employee morale and responds to a crisis using rapid-response techniques comparable to Smokey the Bear and forest firefighters (don't they know that HR can smell the proverbial smoke from miles away?).

You conclude the meeting thinking that this list along with HR's amazing knowledge, skill, and ability (KSA) should guarantee a freaking seat-at-the-table, right? "Yes, unequivocally, without a doubt, absolutely, unquestionably, undeniably, and completely!" says your voice of reason.

Moment of Truth: Because of my years of experience and systematic exposure to the real-life situations that others can't even imagine, I can and have proven to serve as a key contributor to companies in good as well as in challenging times. Make no mistake about it—a seat at the table is not taken lightly. Therefore, those in senior leadership should *not* take having a representative from HR at the table lightly. "Quid pro quo, Clarice" (in my best Hannibal Lector voice from the Academy Award-winning movie *Silence of the Lambs*).

Speaking of movies. The perfect visual of decision-making success for an HR professional can be likened to a scene in a movie when the director yells, "ACTION!" and the CEO's executive assistant begins to take roll of those *invited* and in attendance at the decision-making meeting. The camera pans right, and your name is called as a representative for HR. You do not answer, and the room is eerily silent. Then the organizer yells, "Stop the meeting. I need to call HR before we can move forward!"

But wait ... a good screenplay always has an alternative ending, right? Right! So the camera pans right, and your name is called as a representative for HR. You calmly but enthusiastically say, "Present!" Then the organizer says, "Great, as we couldn't start this meeting without HR!" Now *that's* an Academy Award-winning ending, if I must say so myself.

Fast-Forward: So the moral of this story is that HR professionals put on their pants and skirts, shirts and blouses, shoes and stilettos the exact same way as do executives and senior management. So speak now or forever hold your peace and be missing at the table.

When your name is not called, say it yourself.

5

The HR Wheel

"There's a hole in the middle, in the middle of the wheel, dear Carol, dear Carol ..."

So what is the HR wheel? It is a phrase I personally coined in the latter part of my career after being exposed to the multifaceted roles of HR over the last twenty years. I recently heard a hip-hop song by the artist Drake entitled "Started From the Bottom," and while the majority of the chorus was beyond the context of this book, I could relate to the phrase because I started my HR career from the bottom and have worked my way up the ladder over the last several years. Little did I know, or ever comprehend, that there were so many facets of HR to learn, interpret, and discern to ensure that my peers and the HR industry would accurately designate me as the subject matter expert (SME).

Hence, the HR wheel was born as an illustration in my mind's eye. And based on my experience, each piece of the pie is equal, relevant, and crucial to HR wholeness. The beauty of the HR wheel is that an HR professional can start anywhere on the wheel and go in any direction during his or her career. However, the one prerequisite, in my humble opinion, is that you must truly *love* HR if you are to pursue HR as a career.

HR Wheel

Moment of Truth: My path began as a receptionist who reported to an HR manager. Yes, that's right. My dream was to be an architect, but like they say, "You never know what path your life will take." Hence, my debut in HR (Chapter 10). Back then I was just trying to make a reasonable living and decent salary. But like magic, out of the rainy Seattle skies, the opportunity to relate to people in their time of need and officially join the ranks of the society of HR professionals showered down on me. (Sidebar: HR professionals are dramatic and *love* to use their metaphors and adjectives!) And just like that, an opportunity to serve a company's internal customers was mine for the taking. My first HR mentor (Chapter 2) recognized that I was a natural for a role in HR and believed that I had a knack for relating, communicating, and building relationships with people.

I quickly ascertained that the key to serving in HR is to remember that employees-are-humans seeking support and resources in their time of need. Therefore, I have always engrained in my direct reports two key concepts:

1. Employees are more than just social security numbers and names. They are human beings with families, homes, and bills to pay who are just trying to make a dollar out of fifteen cents. The sooner HR professionals recognize these realities, the more successful and rewarding a career in HR will be.

2. Nothing in HR is black and white; therefore, expect various shades of gray in your HR job, no matter the size of the company. (More like *Fifty Shades of Grey,* but keep it clean people. We are in HR.)

These two realizations engrained in me by my mentors provided a foundation for my HR career and helped me navigate the valleys and plains of HR on a daily basis. I started small by watching and observing HR professionals and progressively was introduced to the real world of HR.

I can confidently declare that I am a walking, talking, living, breathing product of how HR can make a positive impact in an employee's life. My story began in early 1992, when unfortunate circumstances required me to leave the nest of my first HR mentor in Seattle and relocate to my hometown of Denver, Colorado. When I shared the details of my circumstances with my boss and mentor, she listened to my request and immediately identified an opportunity for me in the city I called home. She knew I was seeking shelter from the life and the rain of Seattle and did not hesitate or judge me. Her actions were a true display of empathy, employee relations, and recruiting wrapped into one kind gesture. Right before my eyes, my mentor applied my first HR key concept: Remember, we are all just human beings trying to weather the storms of life. During that transition, "watch and learn" became the first of my many HR mantras.

Upon returning home to the Rocky Mountains and snow-covered pikes, I was gently and responsibly handed over to a new HR mentor who was patient, kind, and just as fantastic. Her professional declaration to me was "I will teach you everything I know in case I am hit by a bus." Sounds morbid and a bit like a bad life insurance claim waiting to happen for those of you who have chosen benefits as your specialty on the HR wheel. But just as it played out in that famous scene in the movie *Forrest Gump*, the bus she spoke of did come, but it didn't stop. As predicted, she was hit by a metaphorical bus in the form of her resignation letter to the company.

After a brief moment of freaking panic, I collected myself, as she told me I could do this, and I became the interim HR manager until a replacement was found. Long story short, I was still a novice in HR, and in that bitter moment, I knew what it felt like to be identified as "underqualified." This term is among the famous last words of HR during the recruiting process and still is used and viewed in museums today near the dinosaur bones.

By this time, I had observed how HR handled employee-relations issues, recruiting strategy, and learning and development plans. And lo and behold, I was the lead actress of this HR feature film. You see, I was trained on the HR fundamentals in the quite untraditional manner we affectionately call "hands-on training." How untraditional, you ask? Well, I was hired and trained to also be the accounts payable clerk as a side role because someone within the company thought the function should report to HR. (Waiting for the freaking laughter ...) While unexplainable, the training and experience I received proved to be extremely beneficial because I added another skill to my resume and had an understanding of the basic finance lingo, such as EBIT, EBITDA, G/L, and overhead expenses.

One year later, I was granted an opportunity to be the HR administrator over the regional location, which was also in Denver. My new role included employee relations, recruiting, and ... wait for it ... procurement! Yes, they snuck in another non-HR task to my job description. But I loved it because I was able to learn the core business. At that moment, I realized the importance of understanding the core business and that it would make a traditional HR professional an FREAKING AMAZING, INNOVATIVE, and TRUSTED member of the company.

Pause Moment: Time to review my HR wheel checklist:

- Employee Relations Relator—Check

- Employee Benefits Specialist—Time to spin the wheel

While I was only allowed to handle the L to Z of benefits administration, I knew I would enjoy learning about this facet of HR. What is the L to Z of benefits administration? Well, I am glad you asked because this is another phrase I coined in my early career. It means to be the receiver of benefit enrollment materials, updates, and communication for dissemination to employees, but not a contributor to the A to K strategic and planning process of benefits administration.

After a couple of years, I had begun to build a pretty solid HR portfolio, as my exposure to compensation and payroll was inevitable in my new HR role. Even before my HR career, my parents and relatives clearly communicated, "We don't work for free so that job better not mess with my money." Translated, this meant that if I didn't accomplish anything else over a one- or two-week timeframe, I better make certain that timecards were processed for the nonexempt-hourly employees and that the auto-pay was on for the exempt-salaried employees.

Before the 1999 D-Day (Oh, never mind. False alarm. We made it to January 1, 2000.), nonexempt-hourly employees submitted paper time sheets and HR entered the hours into the payroll system. The crescendo to all that ten-key data entry you may have been lucky enough to learn in high school typing class was the tangible paper specimen we called a paycheck. Millions of Americans would receive this paper document and rush to the bank during their breaks and lunches to cash or deposit the specimen in hopes that the personal check they wrote two days earlier did not beat them to the bank and do that dance we call *The Bounce*. But all good things must come to an end (*not!*), and the policy announcing voluntary and *mandatory* direct deposit was added to the HR directive. I was among those happy about this technological evolution even if it did cause a temporary revolution amongst the soldiers ... I mean, employees. (See Chapter 3).

Fast-Forward: With the driving force behind an employee paycheck, you can't overlook the importance of needing to understand and conquer the world of compensation. If you thought performance reviews were subjective, then you are in for a bumpy ride in the world of compensation because all employees believe they are worth more than they are paid; hence the highly utilized phrase "underpaid and overworked." While I, too, believe I am worth my secret weight in gold, every competent HR professional knows that a company would go bankrupt trying to pay me and others by the kilo. The reality is that compensation hierarchy and structure is needed in order to manage company overhead, profit margins, and employee expectations. I by no means intend to simplify a very crucial component of my HR wheel in a few sentences, but the truth is that you and others like you will be placed in a box and have to work within these boundaries.

Although you may have been told all your life by those who love (or hate) you that you are unique and special (either in a good or bad way), you will be subjected to the standard base pay structure and offered a fixed salary for performing standard job duties. Your position, most likely, has a minimum- to maximum-level pay range. (Oh, how you pray that you are not at the bottom of that pay range when your offer letter arrives!) Mix in your experience and skill level with competitive industry data based on your geographical area and you have a recipe for a good old-fashioned compensation program. And in order to put the minimum-pay range in your rearview mirror, you must show yourself worthy to earn a salary or merit increase that is achieved through another subjective HR practice called employee performance reviews. (Hold onto your HR hats because this is a chapter in my next series of books.)

Pause Moment: Time to review my HR wheel checklist:

- Employee Relations Relator—Check

- Payroll Gatekeeper—Check

- Compensation Regulator—Check

- Aspiring Employee Benefits Specialist—Spinning

- Workers' Compensation-Storyteller—Spin wheel or get hurt after-hours

After adding a few more years to my HR repertoire, it was time to roll up my shelves and live the life of the rich and famous and navigate the unchartered world of employee benefits. My first dose of reality was when I technically realized the only one who is truly rich or famous in the company is the CEO. I was becoming extremely familiar with that overused term "confidentiality" and could only peep for moment at his salary before thinking that is what I make in an entire year! However, I remembered the code of ethics and the unofficial oath I took sometime during my HR career to safeguard information, and so I sighed and moved on with hope to one day being considered "highly compensated" in the eyes of the IRS. Okay, okay, that was payroll, not benefits. (This moment in my career *still* makes me lose my train of thought.)

So on the of topic employee benefits, when combined with salary, this is why employees consider your company the ever-so-famous "employer of choice." And this is the part of my story where I began to learn the A to K of benefits administration. Yes, I was now a contributor to the A to K strategic and planning process of benefits plan administration! So what does strategy and benefits have in common, and why do we need to plan? Don't the benefits offered by the company magically appear for employees to choose from during that time of year called open enrollment? Negative, Captain. It is not that simple!

This is when I quickly learned that company size, demographics (e.g., age and gender), and past plan utilization and history play a large part in the affordability of the benefits that are offered as a group health plan. I also learned that this process is the tip of the iceberg, and that there is much more ice under the waterline I would have to learn and interpret if I was to provide the company with a comprehensive benefit plan that employees would value and could afford on a pre-tax basis. As a reminder, pre-tax benefits are probably the only shelter from the storms of life that employees will receive from the government (in the form of a tax shelter). Again, this component of HR can't be described in a few sentences, but it has had the most impact in my career. I truly believe the mastery of this facet has allowed me to help the greatest number of people, which is what HR is all about. Helping people decode the benefits matrix and getting to wear that cool black leather trench coat Morpheus wore in *The Matrix* was my dream.

So let's cut (pun intended) from the benefit matrix to the tales of workplace injuries and workers' compensation. I sometimes liken workers' compensation to the Wild Wild West because the incident reports outlining how workplace injuries occurred were amongst some of the wildest stories I have ever heard in my career. For instance, one time a female employee was attempting to lift a frozen deer, which was to be kept for future testing in our environmental laboratory, onto a truck bed, when she was inadvertently pinned under the animal when the heave-ho went wrong. Yes, this was a real freaking story, and I will bet my HR allowance that HR professionals near and far have similar bizarre and crazy stories like this one. (Oh, if the walls and file cabinets could talk, what stories they would tell!) On a more serious note, no HR professional wants to receive a report regarding an injured employee. The reality is that while some may be minor, others are serious and life threatening, so the true name of this game is prevention under the watchful eye of the Occupational

Safety and Health Administration (OSHA), also known as OH ... NO.

An HR professional's ability to manage an injury incident from beginning to end is a display of patience and collaboration at its finest. The ability to record facts related to an incident like a detective from an episode of *Perry Mason* is an art *and* science because somehow the story from the injured employee is not always the same the second time it's told or described by witnesses (if you are lucky enough to have one or two). While the goal is to ensure the employee seeks and obtains immediate medical attention, a telephone call to the company's workers' compensation provider is next on the list so the events are recorded for the road to rehabilitation, or Maximum Medical Improvement (MMI).

MMI is defined by the Workers' Compensation Institute (2013) as the point at which the injured worker's medical condition has stabilized and further functional improvement is unlikely, despite continued medical treatment or physical rehabilitation. MMI is the term injured employees dread and the status for which companies target. The key to properly managing a workers' compensation claim is patience and time because the clock runs on a different time zone with each case. The optimal outcome is the return to work of the injured employee to the same job duties. Although this status is possible, this outcome is definitely one for the HR record books, if achieved. Hence, the role of a highly skilled HR professional, who can take a great deal of the credit for these successes no matter how farfetched the details of the incidents.

Moment of Truth: While serving as a benefits and workers' compensation manager, I was subjected to incidents that only a sense of humor could navigate, for the reality was that the MMI for some of my cases was they would never work again. This sparked my next HR mantra, "Help is hope and sometimes that's all you can give."

Pause Moment: Time to review my HR wheel checklist:

- Employee Relations Relator—Check
- Payroll Gatekeeper—Check
- Compensation Regulator—Check
- Aspiring Employee Benefits Specialist—Check
- Optimism-Laced Workers' Compensation—Check
- Organizational Development Makeover—Spin the almighty wheel.

Fast-Forward: Let us now transition to organizational development (OD), which ranks right up there with the heavyweight champions of the world. HR professionals who put their hats in the ring for OD are requesting to test their agility and knowledge of the company and HR. Let's start with the fact that OD has numerous, but similar, definitions and can be likened to the Oracle in *The Matrix*, the Great and Powerful Oz in *The Wizard of Oz*, or Charlie from the seventies hit television series *Charlie's Angels*. One classic definition of organizational development comes from Richard Beckhard's 1969 book *Organization Development: Strategies and Models*:

Organization Development is an effort (1) planned, (2) organization-wide, and (3) managed from the top, to (4) increase organization effectiveness and health through (5) planned interventions in the organizations "processes," using behavioral-science knowledge.

A slightly different definition comes from Matt Minahan at MM & Associates, in Silver Spring, Maryland, a leader in the OD network:

Organization Development is a body of knowledge and practice that enhances organizational performance and individual development, by increasing alignment among the various systems within the overall system. OD interventions are inclusive methodologies and approaches to strategic planning, organization design, leadership development, change management, performance management, coaching, diversity, team building, and work/life balance.

So now that the function of OD is clear as mud (but probably not), I will share my favorite simplistic definition outlined in the book *Health Behavior and Health Education: Theory, Research, and Practice*, Fourth Edition, which sounds more like a mission statement of sorts but provides the insight needed to understand that mastering OD can make a good HR professional GREAT (in my favorite Jack Welch voice):

Organizational Development (OD) is a field of research, theory, and practice dedicated to expanding the knowledge and effectiveness of people to accomplish more successful organizational change and performance.

Moment of Truth: I was privileged to work with, and observe, some of the best in HR as they maneuvered through the OD stages. I even freaking helped my team reach set milestones along the way. I admired them for knowing upfront that the first stage is inevitably the chaos stage, and everyone had a firefighter mentality despite the best HR therapy sessions. I actively participated in efforts to help them reach the second stage: stability, and supported the back-to-basics philosophy. And as it goes with all great HR initiatives, I celebrated with them when they reached the third and final stage: high performance, which meant they had reached and attained the outstanding, sustainable results the company desired, affectionately referred to as esprit de corp.[12]

Pause Moment: Time to review my HR wheel checklist ...

- Employee Relations Relator—Check

- Payroll Gatekeeper—Check

- Compensation Regulator—Check

- Aspiring Employee Benefits Specialist—Check

- Optimism-Laced Workers' Compensation—Check

- Organizational Development Makeover—Check

- Recruiting Mr. and Ms. Right—Spin the wheel

Fast-Forward: Now that I have outlined the secret to becoming an HR sensei master of OD, let's spend the last moment of this chapter outlining why recruiting makes the world of HR go 'round. Recruiting. Just the word can make a seasoned HR professional say, "I have done my time" or an aspiring HR professional say, "I need to put in my time if I am to play with the big girls and boys." As the well-respected amphibian, Kermit the Frog, would say, "It's not easy being a recruiter."

The day begins and ends with the same directive: identify candidates who have the KSAs needed to fill open positions within a company. A recruiter's life includes ongoing discussions with hiring managers and executives in search of the perfect candidate who will be the solution to all their problems for at least one day. Then they are on to the next candidate. Yes, this sounds a bit like playing the field even before the ink is dry on the marriage license ... I mean, offer letter. But this is the reality recruiters are faced with because everyone needs that perfect candidate whose skills match the job description *now*, not later.

Moment of Truth: I remember being tasked with recruiting international nurses during my tenure at a Texas-based hospital in the early 2000s. The job description outlined the basic skills, licenses, and certifications "preferred, but not required." (I have heard that catchphrase a million and one times and still believe it is just marshmallow language.) However, the two attributes not listed, but made very clear to me during my search, were courage and bravery.

After my second or third telephone interview, I had to have tissue nearby, as these nurses shared stories of protecting patients from militant guerilla soldiers who had invaded the hospital while nurses were caring for patients or rendering aid to ailing children in third world countries where access to trained physicians and medical supplies was extremely limited. I am grateful for this experience and proud to have been tasked with overseeing and participating in the recruiting responsibilities.

Fast-Forward: Recruiters really do make the world go 'round, as they are considered the receptionists of the HR industry. They are the first impression a person has of the company and its culture and are charged with making a lasting impression on the qualified candidate who may, in the end, be "the one" ... if even for a short while. So run, don't walk, to the concession stand at the next SHRM conference and buy the bumper sticker that says, "Don't forget to kiss your recruiter TODAY!"

Final Pause Moment (in this chapter anyway): Time to review my HR wheel checklist ...

- Employee Relations Relator—Check

- Payroll Gatekeeper—Check

- Compensation Regulator—Check

- Aspiring Employee Benefits Specialist—Check

- Optimism-Laced Workers' Compensation—Check

- Organizational Development Makeover—Check

- Recruiting Mr. and Ms. Right—Check

So the checklist is complete, and as you can see, the HR wheel captures the multiple facets of a well-rounded HR professional. While those in non-HR roles may call HR professionals L7-squares rather than well-rounded, I can with a high degree of confidence, say that no matter what my shape or their perception, I feel as though I have made a difference in the lives of employees and companies that strive to be the best. So while my life in HR may have not been viewed as glamorous, I feel like a star when I am called on to serve in any of the facets in my HR wheel. It's also my hope that HR professionals who are reading this book will too. Spin on, my friends!

Your career is your palette,
so paint with a broad brush and lots of color.

6

HR, Employee Relations or Relationships with Employees?

As an HR professional, day after day I ask myself, "Are we responsible for employee relations or relationships with employees? Or *both*?" These questions may result in a momentary pause as you raise a finger to your lips and enter into deep thought to ponder the answer.

I therefore believe it is important to start with some background on how HR is perceived (which we will address again and again and again during our journey together). According to my research, it perceivably started as far back as the days of personnel.

Personnel [ˌpər-sə-ˈnel]

NOUN:

1. The body of one person employed by or active in a organizations business or service.

2. The department of human resources in an organization.

3. An administrative division of an organization concerned with the body of person employee by or active in it and often acting as a liaison between different departments.[13]

If we properly dissect this definition, today's HR professionals were forged from the yesteryear definition of personnel. Even when we look back, the primary objective of our HR ancestors was to take care of people. So despite the date and year on your desk calendar, the role of HR was, and still is, to connect with the humans, who we label as employees on a daily basis.

Although the definition describes personnel as the liaison between departments, HR professionals are also affectionately known to employees near and far as their confidant and voice of reason. During our time of service, we have talked numerous employees and managers off the proverbial ledge, cliff, or bridge. We have even been asked to intervene and mediate when discussions in the workplace have taken a turn for the worst. Our telephone numbers and work extensions are on speed dial on the phones of employees, managers, and executives alike. We are expected to drop *everything* at a moment's notice and resolve issues that no mortal could resolve. Okay, okay, I got carried away, but it feels like that from time to time, right? The point is, we have one job title listed on our business card, but written in pen, pencil, marker, or crayon is a long list of aliases and AKAs.

ABC Company, Inc.

ABC Company, Inc.
123 Save Me Blvd.
There For You, Texas
USA
1-800-HELPMENOW

Carol McBride, PHR, SHRM-CP
VP Human Resources
Voice of Reason
Mediator
Lifesaver
Problem Solver
Superhero
Referee
Coach

During the golden age of personnel, our HR ancestors were, at times, guilty of assimilating employees to just a list of names and social security numbers (or whatever the government identification is in your country). The good news is that HR evolution was inevitable and this archaic perception of employees could not survive the sophistication and complexities of business strategy. However, until then, the role of HR was to answer general personnel questions about labor relations, timekeeping, workers' compensation, and compliance (AKA policy police). Employees would march down to the personnel department with hopes of obtaining answers to their questions during fifteen-minute breaks or before or after their shifts. HR would answer their questions after briefly requesting them to state their name and social security or employee number.

Nope, the Social Security Number Privacy Act and Identity Theft Prevention Act of 2009 were far from enactment because those bad people who steal identities had not yet been granted access to the revolutionary technology called the World Wide Web.

By no means is this an attempt to downgrade the role of our HR ancestors, for it was their strong, broad shoulders that carried HR to the evolution stage. Their dedication to the craft of HR kept us from going extinct and opened the door to those who would answer the call to serve as an HR professional in this new era. It is fitting that we now pause for a moment to say thank you to all the domestic and international personnel professionals.

Richard M. Vosburgh, SVP-HR of MGM and Mirage Properties, best describes the road forward in his article entitled, "The Evolution of HR: Developing HR as an Internal Consulting Organization":

> Together and now, business leaders and HR professionals have the opportunity to understand the history that brings us to our current situation, to be informed by predictable trends, and to make the transformation necessary to result in organizational competitive advantage and HR functional viability.[14]

I laughingly believe the call to arms occurred when HR was summoned by the all-knowing HR Oracle and told that HR must progressively move from being known as the day-to-day administrative expert to an employee-relations and change-agent expert with the ultimate goal of blossoming into a strategic HR and business partner of the company. (By the way, no one really knows who the HR Oracle is because of a signed confidentiality agreement dating back to when God created the heavens and the earth.) In addition to this directive, HR was advised to always remember on which side its bread was buttered and thereby understand that *relationships with employees* must remain the center of its focus.

Today, HR has evolved and so have the relationships with employees. They have moved beyond seeking our advice regarding general questions and now seek our insight on issues with a greater level of complexity. This new type of relationship allows you, the HR professional, to finally get the opportunity to exercise those techniques you learned from courses like *The Speed of Trust* (2006) created by Stephen Covey. This course states that if employees are to trust HR, the following Four Cores of Credibility must be evident:

- Integrity—Do you walk your talk and will you stand up for what is right?

- Intent—Do you care and will you act in an employee's best interest?

- Capabilities—Do you have the KSAs that will ensure you are equipped to address even the most complex issues?

- Results—What is your track record and will it breed positive "trust dividends"?

This course also emphasizes that achieving credibility and high trust are key to effectively managing employee issues because not all outcomes are easy or end favorably. However, navigating through the issues without compromising your credibility, trust, and integrity with employees is a win for HR as a whole.

So referencing those technique flash cards and books whenever possible is a good thing to do to stay on pace, for just as you settle into your stride, you will inevitably come face-to-face with an employee seeking guidance on how to deal with another issue, such as how to deal with a difficult supervisor. This new issue will also allow you to use those techniques you learned during a course similar to that of the Fierce Conversations (Fierce, Inc., 2007) that was recommended by the company's learning and development

(L&D) director. One of the three transformational ideas stated in that course is that during a difficult or fierce conversation, "the conversation is the relationship" and provides a helpful tip to be shared with employees faced with manager-communication issues. The course fundamentals are a reminder to HR professionals to advise employees to eighty-six any solutions that involve smacking their supervisor and recommend that they, politely and respectfully, ask their manager for what they need in terms of feedback, direction, and support to be successful.

Unfortunately, inquiries and calls for help with these types of employee-relations issues become progressively more complex and frequent. HR must hold fast to the commitment we made to uphold the promise of an open-door policy ... rather than darting from our desks and closing the office door in hopes no one else will knock.

So what exactly do I mean by "complex HR issue"? Well, such an issue may begin when an allegation of discrimination or sexual harassment in the workplace, which is communicated to HR on the record. For the record, there is no such thing as an off-the-record conversation with employees in HR, so make sure you strike this phrase from the vocabulary of entry-level HR professionals and employees. Use your skills and trust to explain how you would handle the details of the conversation rather than saying yes to an off-the-record conversation.

Your comprehensive knowledge about how to handle these types of claims will remind you how important integrity, credibility, and a good track record related to trust will be under these circumstances. The sensitive nature of such allegations will require you to put on your employee relations hat, and your thorough understanding of employment law and policy will be crucial to navigating through the shocking facts of the claim. You may secretly wish there was a map with driving directions to the final destination, but you know that the GPS will misguide you because of all the new roads ... I mean, rulings ... that have set precedence since the enactment of Title VII of the Civil Rights Act of 1964. Yep, that was almost six decades ago, and lots of things have changed, but this act still says this type of behavior in the workplace is prohibited.

You also must not allow your pride or prejudice to get in the way of initiating "Project Sounding Board," a play right out of the merger-and-acquisition playbook and code for "contact your employment law legal counsel immediately." Recognize that sometimes you just need a neutral party to discuss the facts of the allegation, one who has not been onsite witnessing this season's episode of *Employees Gone Wild*.

During discrimination and harassment investigations, your efforts will require patience, and when you run out of patience, you will have to dig deep for more patience. And just when that supply is depleted, you will have to pray for even *more* patience and hope that missing church or Mass last Sunday will not destroy your chances of God hearing and answering your prayer. Once you have patience as a virtue, you can add your solid employee-relations track record and thus increase your chances for an amicable final decision that will help the company limit or mitigate legal liability. Executive leadership may even nominate you for the annual Lifesaver Award, for your thorough investigation and decisive action may have salvaged the credibility of the company even though the claim had a black-box warning label on it from the start.

BLACK BOX WARNINGS

HR and legal counsel will recommend that this sexual discrimination claim carry a **black box warning** on the file to indicate that opening this file could increase the risk of panic, shock or shame. Explanations from both parties will be drastically different. There will be two sides to the story, which will have a side effect of confusion and require a great deal of patience to address.

- **Unwelcome Sexual Advances**
  (marketed as "welcomed")

- **Verbal Harassment**
  (marketed as "got it on tape")

- **Requests for Sexual Favors**
  (marketed as "it was a favor")

- **Offensive Remarks**
  (marketed as "trash talk")

Once the smoke clears from black box issues such as these, you can take an Olympic deep breath and say to yourself, I think I have reached my quota for the year, and then secretly wish you could run an ad in the company newsletter that reads, "Keep your hands to yourself! And if you don't have anything nice to say, then don't say anything at all!"

But you know your wish is a pipe dream, so you do the next best thing—schedule mandatory harassment training for the entire company. Let the complaining begin because everyone will claim, "It will never happen to me" or "I would never be accused of harassment." Yep, denial is real, and you are going to help them with this misconception and have them sign a form acknowledging they understand once the training is over. This is HR in action. You recommend that everyone watch and learn because you are addressing the needs of the company proactively rather than on a reactionary basis. Admit it … these are HR tactics at their finest.

Moment of Truth: I have conducted many of these investigations in my career, and each one was challenging and disturbing. I devoted time to ensuring I completed a thorough investigation despite how gruesome and heartrending the circumstances. Many times, the victims were distraught and shared stories that had taken a toll on them mentally. They could no longer take the harassment or discrimination and had reached their proverbial breaking point. I heard the cries, literally and figuratively, and had an obligation to respond and investigate. I realized that these situations were no laughing matter, but during the conversations with the victims, I found that they had lives beyond the job and discussions of things that brought them happiness brought about smiles that took some of the power away from the perpetrator. From these conversations, I forged positive relationships with employees and built trust that they still thank me for today.

I wished that these allegations had not brought us to this point, rather than considering the initial reason we all were brought together, which was to work, not harass or treat people differently because of their race, religion, gender, or physical impairments. After all, doesn't the second paragraph in the Declaration of Independence state, "We hold these truths to be self-evident, that all Men are created equal, that they are endowed by their Creator with certain unalienable Rights, that among these are Life, Liberty, and the Pursuit of Happiness"? Unfortunately, some people didn't get the Declaration of Independence memo HR added to their new-hire packet, so now evasive action is required.

Fast-Forward: HR saves the day *again* under extremely tedious circumstances that require the extraordinary ability to navigate the employee-relations issue while forging positive and trusting relationships with employees. So the answer to our questions at the beginning of this chapter is a resounding "BOTH!" I can sincerely say I am proud to be amongst the hundreds of thousands of HR professionals who stand up for what is right and work day after day to restore order even when the circumstances are freaking crummy.

Relations may be temporary,
but relationships are built to last.

7
Mergers and Acquisitions: When Were You Going to Tell HR?

The day starts like any other day ... or so you think. But the doors in the executive corridor begin to close more frequently and chatter amongst in-house general counsel increases significantly, and not because of the employee disciplinary issue you discussed last week. (Thank God *that's* over.)

At that moment, you recall the countless number of meetings your CEO/president attended about a month ago and the flurry of black suits that were escorted to the large executive conference room. You then begin to piece together the timeline of events in your mind, like a good HR professional does (we call it the HR Spidey sense). You know this activity can only be about one of three things:

1. Merger.

2. Acquisition.

3. Layoffs.

4. Divestiture.

(Oh, that is four things ... never said we were good at math ... but we are darn good at reading people!)

Your thoughts then turn for a brief moment to ponder how these discussions may have started. You recall the circumstances surrounding the last deal, and you begin to laugh uncontrollably. You and your colleagues knew it as "the napkin deal." Yes, the rumors were true. The CEO/president had what was supposed to be a casual dinner with another executive from a company with a similar business portfolio, and during their dining experience (and after the second drink), they had a brilliant idea. The conversation went something like this:

- Merger: "Let's join forces" (*Marvel Comics* Wonder Twins style).

- Acquisition: "Business hasn't been good. It's time to consider financial offers to sell."

Your CEO/president then reached for the napkin that had not yet been saturated by the condensation from his third drink and began to sketch out a plan for a potential M&A deal. Both parties closely reviewed the napkin through cocktail eyes, and then—*BAM!*—the napkin was initialed and the deal to begin the process of acquiring company XYZ was done. Your CEO/president folded the napkin and placed it in his inside jacket pocket, and dinner was served. The next day, the napkin resurfaced in the general counsel and COO's office and the due diligence discussion began.

But then you remember how the due diligence efforts really played out on that fateful, groundbreaking day. In fact, you distinctly remember it played out *without* HR being informed or alerted of the impending acquisition of company XYZ. "What the freaking jelly beans is the matter with these people?" is the only narrative you can muster up as you refrain from spewing other expletives.

The impending acquisition was even given the covert operation name of Project Magellan to keep details of the activity secret. All you could think then was, where the jumping Jehoshaphat do they come up with these names? Didn't they Google details pertaining to Magellan? Don't they realize that Magellan was struck and killed by a poisoned bamboo spear and later surrounded and finished off with other weapons toward the end of his journey around the world? Great, an M&A project named after an explorer who died at the end of his journey.

"Brace yourself" is all you can say to yourself now and make a note to yourself: "Be proactive. Provide a list of birds for the next potential M&A effort and advise to ditch the explorer-naming scheme."

But no worries, right? If it smells like money and better profit margins, what can go wrong, right?

WRONG!

The reality was the freight train was on the tracks, and nothing would stop or derail Project Magellan (not even a bamboo spear). Or so they thought.

A few days later, and unbeknownst to HR, general counsel from both companies began to discuss the following objectives of the M&A,[15] of which I have taken the liberty to translate with a sense of humor:

1. Define the merger and acquisition. (Remind me why we are doing this again?)

2. List twelve conditions required to merge. (That could take all day. Did someone order lunch?)

3. Define and perform due diligence. (Should we call HR yet? Nah!)

4. Identify information to consider before "doing a deal". (Too late!)

5. Describe antitrust guidelines. (Trust me, it will be

okay!)

6. Explain M&A percent rules. (Didn't we agree on 95/5 during dinner? That's translation for "Darn near absolute control.")

7. Plan for merger and acquisition of two companies. (Details, details! Maybe we should call HR now? Nah!)

8. Decide on acquisition terms. (It's our way or the highway, buddy!)

9. List factors in determining a price. (I thought we agreed upon one dollar. Or was that after the third drink at dinner?)

10. Describe grading criteria. (On a scale of 1 to 10, I am a 10, baby! No need to look at my measurements on Dun & Bradstreet.)

11. Summarize acquisition strategy and process. (You show me yours and I'll show you mine!)

12. Finance the merger. (Would you like that all in ones or twenties?)

13. Describe the risk of the acquisition. (Trust me, you have *nothing* to worry about!)

14. Explain the methods of hostile takeover bids. (So you are just going to go over my head to the shareholders? I thought we were better than that?)

15. Outline Securities and Exchange Commission (SEC) filing requirements and tax considerations. (Who called the SEC??)

16. Enumerate defensive measures by targeted company (Anyone got a golden parachute in their office?).

17. Describe accounting, reporting, and disclosures for business combinations. (Show me the numbers!)

Wow! Despite this extensive list, there are no references to employees or any of the following critical HR due diligence deliverables:

- A workforce census. (Knowing your people is the name of the game.)

- A list of all employment contracts. (Who was promised heaven on Earth?).

- List of employee benefits plan. (Better known as hidden surprises in the cereal box.).

- Employee compliance documents, e.g. I-9, W-2. (We don't want no problems with the government.).

- Workplace investigation files. (Unsolved and unresolved mysteries.).

You are now inwardly screaming and yelling, "Who's freaking in *charge*?" Yep, that is why they should have called HR at the revealing of the napkin gala. SMH!

Must we publish an HR advisory on the importance of change management and communication strategy with employees as the focal point? Must we remind executives that even the whisper of a merger or acquisition can set the rumor mill on fire or into overdrive like the script of one of those new feature films ending in numbers six, seven, or eight (or whichever sequel they are on now)?

Studies have shown that rumors in the workplace can lead to an unhealthy work environment, so it is critical to make sure it does not occur. Take a look at how often employees engage in gossip and spread rumors at work.

According to the blog *People Communicating* the main reason people spread rumors is because they feel "anxious or stressed out" and spreading rumors "is a way of making sense of a stressful situation."[16] Hence, the business case for HR's involvement at the beginning of the due diligence discussion. Allowing HR to be proactive with a well-crafted communication and change-management strategy can reduce and manage stress and relieve anxiety. News flash: to merge with or acquire a company means you need to come away with the workforce intact, not shattered like pieces of glass for HR to pick up. So why not allow HR to proactively implement a retention plan or retain a recruiter to assist with replacing the defectors who could disrupt the productivity of the company? This would result in fewer cuts to bandage and decrease the number of calls from senior management requesting that HR help "stop the bleeding."

How Often People Spread Rumors at Work

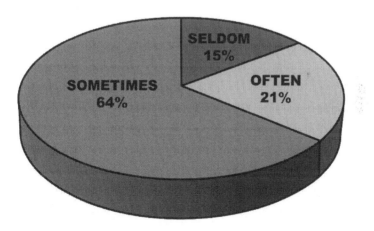

Make no mistake: this is not a dig at executives because we … meaning HR … get it. In the end, it's about preparing for the probability of rumors and workforce disruption and reassuring the current workforce of job stability. The lesson to be learned from this story is to remember to call HR when the decision is made to acquire or merge with another company. We are simply asking the C-suite to pick up the phone, walk down the hall, take the elevator, or send a smoke signal to HR at the beginning, not when the credits are rolling at the end. HR is here to help you and the company. We don't mind being nominated for supporting actress or actor rather than the leading roles. HR wants to be the voice carrying the message of:

- Facts

- Expectations

- Reassurance

- Clarity

- Impact

- Honesty

- Empathy

- Success

During M&As, employees rely on HR and senior executives to uphold the promise of transparency and being forthcoming about the fate of the company. Hearing about the details of an M&A at the watercooler with the company's busybody is sure to be laced with embellishments and a half cup of truth. Even worse is having your employees turn on the television and hear about this important development on the news or via a financial blog or newsfeed. Even though HR has grown accustomed to dispatching people who specialize in damage control, watercooler rumors and the local news are not the preferred starting points for the company M&A. These methods of communication are surefire ways of increasing employee turnover.

Need more convincing? The Center for American Progress estimates that it costs one-fifth of a new recruit's annual salary to replace a lost employee. They also estimate that private industry cost for the loss of employees in highly skilled jobs cost up to 213 percent of the new position's annual salary.[17] Need one more freaking statistic to drive this point home? According to SHRM's Human Capital Benchmarking database, annual turnover rate averages 15 percent across all industries.[18]

So what is the solution when HR's chair is empty at the decision-making meetings? Smacking some freaking sense into the C-suite sounds nice, but promoting violence in the workplace is not the right solution and is against company policy. The drawing back of the arm and hand and quickly releasing it could result in HR having to terminate HR, and we just don't like this one bit. So the suggested *nonviolent* recommendation is to present a business case with qualitative and quantitative details and data that will justify inclusion in the early need-to-know stages of an M&A initiative. This approach will require confidence and access to turnover, presenteeism, absenteeism, and employee satisfaction statistics and analytics. They say numbers never lie unless it is bad data, and our fellow HRIS gurus are all too familiar with this issue. Coming to the table armed with this information is like being a part of the main course during dinner and will increase your chances of being invited to stay for dessert, coffee, and perhaps a good cigar—if you are lucky.

When your voice can't be heard, use a megaphone.

8

HR, No Such Thing as a Typical Day

Let's be honest. Can a person really say the words "human resources" and "typical day" in the same sentence without breaking out in uncontrollable laughter? However, once stark reality takes the place of a brief moment of humor, the answer from HR professionals, gurus, and subject-matter experts around the globe is a resounding "NO" in all languages.

The first fact to check is that a standard workday in HR is not a typical eight-hour day. For HR professionals, the day may start well before most people are awake and rubbing the accumulation of tears from their eyes. For starters, it is usually 5:00 a.m. when an HR professional grabs the mobile device of the company's choice from the nightstand. (Note to management: Although HR has a tremendous respect for information technology (IT), devices with roll balls and antennas or that flip open should not be stocked or distributed any longer. Also, research on who has a data tower near the corporate and regional offices would be much appreciated before we are asked to be on call and available day and night. No dig. I am just saying, "*Please*, and thank you!")

Okay, back to 5:00 a.m. The checking of e-mails from the night before begins. Yes, the night before. All HR professionals know that trouble brews the best at night. They don't call it "dead time" on the highly acclaimed sitcom *Paranormal State* for nothing. This is the time when demons and troublemakers come out and think about how they have been wronged, mistreated, misunderstood, and falsely accused by one or several of their coworkers.

Wow. It's now only 5:30, but it is not unusual, or too early, for a horror story to unfold. To deal with this paranormal activity, HR professionals have become like behavioral profilers and can review and discern if urgency is required and whether Ghostbuster suits will be a part of their wardrobe for the day. The trick is to determine if the issue has even a twinge of truth or validity and can be classified as a false-positive and handled later in the not-so-typical day.

By 6:00, the to-do list you compiled the day before is just a distant memory because of the numerous e-mails and voicemails you reviewed over the last hour.

By 7:30, because you are a workaholic, you are in your office and determining the game plan for the day. You truly have only thirty minutes to get it together and gather your

thoughts because the open door policy for the HR department will be in full effect at 8:00 a.m. You curse the man or woman who came up with the darn phrase "open door policy" as well as the person who suggested the company add it to employee handbooks and finally the one who made it the unofficial calling card of HR. You quickly discovered that even with the door closed, employees still knock or abruptly open the door, ignoring that it is closed for a reason.

By 9:00, you have received three employee disciplinary telephone calls from managers for:

- Tardiness.

- Excessive Absenteeism.

- Sexual Harassment. (Ugh, Charlie Brown. Not today. Didn't we say we met our quota for this year?)

Now add two visits from employees who happen to wander by and just want to be nosy, and you are officially off to a not-so-typical day in HR.

Your notebook is filled with facts, accusations, hearsay, and demands by 10:00. You consider if you should go to the restroom or delay your bio-break until lunchtime because you know that the five minutes it would take to accomplish this task could be used to solve a problem or set the wheels in motion for resolution of another problem, "including but up to termination of employment!" **Pause Moment:** My spin on this HR phrase is an inside joke that only HR professionals can relate to, so don't hesitate to pause and call a friend in HR.

You, however, remember that you really need to take bio-breaks in order to avoid other health issues. You think to yourself that your dedication is amazing and run, not walk, to the restroom, barely making it—all in the name of dedication.

By 11:30, you have a completed disciplinary template for the two employees and had a preliminary meeting with inside general counsel on the topic of potential sexual harassment for the third. You have reviewed that darn employee handbook five times and even pulled the employee's file to confirm that he signed the handbook receipt and acknowledgment form during his new-hire orientation. You can't drop the Wile E. Coyote anvil on him if your HR team did not obtain the signed document from the employee. (By the way, Advil is definitely on the menu if you ever get to take a lunch.) Oh, how you cringe when you have this type of case, but that is why they pay you the big bucks, right? Wrong again! (This is the topic of a future chapter on pay equity and equality.)

It is now noon and lunchtime for a typical employee. But not you. This is the only time you have to look at that to-do list you crafted the day before. The following list is long, but the good news is that the tasks are textbook HR that you could complete in your sleep because of your years of experience in HR:

- Offer letters.

- Reference check.

- Schedule performance reviews.

- Review leave of absence request.

- Salary review/benchmarking for potential offer.

- Termination letter.

- Promotion letter.

You are forced to use your prioritization skills you obtained from the numerous seminars you have attended in your career, and by 1:00, you have completed the three most time-sensitive tasks. How did you determine the priority? By date? Nope! Sensitivity? Nope! By which manager was screaming the loudest? Yep! Whoever said HR is a science and not an art was wrong.

At 1:05, you check to see if the coast is clear and make a break for the cafeteria, only to be stopped on the way by another employee who says she only has one "quick" question for you. Yeah, right. Where have you heard *that* before?

You convince her to walk with you and talk along the way, as you are dying of malnutrition. Hell, you are *starving* and can barely focus, but like a true HR professional, you manage to focus, despite the hunger pangs, and proceed to answer all 20 questions.

When you finally arrive at the cafeteria, the special of the day is sold out and nothing is left except for a sad chef salad, but to you it looks like steak, so you take it. You decide to eat the steak … I mean, salad … in your office with the door closed. (Sorry, open door policy. But hunger has triumphed.)

By 1:45, you feel guilty that your door is closed, even though you are eating, so you open it with remnants of salad in your teeth and hope nobody committed a heinous crime during the last twenty minutes.

By 2:00, your computer chimes, alerting you of an internal HR meeting, and you remember it's in the north building, which is four minutes away on a good day. Well, since today is a *bad* day, it is five minutes away because you are *not* going to freaking rush.

You arrive at 2:05, as expected, and everyone looks just as crazy and tattered as you do. You all sigh with relief, acknowledging that you are not alone in this not-so-typical day, and the meeting begins.

The VP of HR starts by saying, "What I am about to share is confidential and is not to leave this room," and you finally have your long-awaited "Ahhh sh*t" moment (outwardly silent but loudly in your head). You think, Can this day get any worse? And then … wait for it—*BAM!*— "Whoop, there it is" (in my best hip-hop rapper Tag Team voice). The VP says, "We are going to have to coordinate a reduction in force [i.e., layoff, downsize, streamline] in sixty days." Your mind is racing and shouting obscenities in French all while she is explaining this nonsense because just six months ago you "facilitated" a napkin acquisition of another company with two hundred employees.

You think to yourself, This hasn't been a typical day, month, year, or *life* as of today. But you signed on to serve the people the HR community calls human capital, so freaking suck it up. A great and motivational way to end this chapter would be to say, "Now the day is over." But since it's *not* a typical day in HR, you must forge on, wear the veil of silence and discretion, and not compromise the confidential information you have just received.

It is now 3:30. As the conference room door opens, you pull your shoulders back to avoid any obvious body language that might start the employee rumor mill and cotton gin. You want to maintain your composure, but you know that someone's fate and livelihood will be changed forever based on the information you just received.

As you walk back to your office, you remember you chose HR as a career because you wanted to help people untangle the complexities of human resources on a not-so-typical day. You also remember just how emotional any given day can be in this role. You run through your credentials in your mind on the five-minute walk back to your office and never come across a degree in psychology, but somehow you feel like you earned it with every termination and layoff. But upon arrival back to your office, you remember that you are the messenger and must deliver whatever news with compassion and empathy so the receiver of the information departs with dignity and pride intact so they may live to fight another day, despite your company's business strategy and directives.

Moment of Truth: Flashback to 1999 and the day you were tasked with flying into a city that didn't know your name or the reason for your visit, contrary to the theme song for the hit television sitcom *Cheers*. Your task was to layoff 20 percent of the workforce at that location because of slumping profitability numbers. Only two people were aware of your arrival and agenda, the worksite operations manager and the foreman. You sat alone in the parking lot in a rental car, looking at the list of names and trying to imagine their responses as you shared the news that they were being terminated. You wondered if they would react with anger, sorrow, or sheer astonishment and possibly perceive your actions as a personal attack rather than you doing your job. Then the adage "Don't shoot the messenger" crossed your mind. After you pondered the figurative and literal concept, you shouted, "Snap out of it. You have a job to do, and you must be mentally strong for them."

You actually opened four doors before the process began: the door to your rental car, the door to the office, the door to the conference room, and the door to your heart and mind, praying that you would deliver the message with the heart of Rachel (notable woman in the Bible), that is, with dignity, grace, gentleness, and kindness.

It began when you asked the operations manager to call in the first employee and you experienced a range of emotions. But halfway through your delivery of the message, along with the severance agreement, the employee said, "Thank you for coming and personally delivering this message and for helping me fulfill my dreams."

What? Your mind went bonkers. You couldn't believe what you were hearing and you wondered if you were on *Candid Camera* as you looked around for a camera. The employee went on to explain, "With this money, now I can fulfill my dreams of starting my own landscaping and gardening business. I have wanted to strike out on my own for so long but was too scared to take a chance on my dream." You maintained your composure and wished him the best, but inwardly you shed a tear and thanked God for the affirmation that your visit mattered and your "living will not be in vain," to borrow a popular line from the old Mahalia Jackson gospel song, "If I Can Help Somebody."

Fast-Forward: You bow your head once before snapping to attention. You reassure yourself that it will be okay, and that you now have a blueprint for your next journey and will stay true to your HR beliefs and foundation. You look at the clock. It is 4:30, and you can hear the quitting-time chatter in the hallway. You check e-mails and the dreaded to-do list; there are over one hundred unopened e-mails, and you have only crossed off half of the items on your list. You take a deep breath and begin to organize your e-mail, searching for words like "urgent," "confidential," or "HELP ME!" You reprioritize your to-do list as best you can, knowing that chances are slim that you will complete the remaining items tomorrow, but you remain cautiously hopeful.

One last glance at the clock reveals it is now 6:00. You click "logoff" on your computer, reach in your desk drawer for your personal belongings, rise from your ergonomic chair, and call it a day ... or ... not-so-typical day in HR.

When the day turns dark,
turn on a light to see your way through.

9

HR, The Motivation Factory

As an HR professional, think of all the millions of employees who arrive to work every day in search of three things:

1. Compensation in exchange for work: "I am not just working for my health. Pay me."

2. Job satisfaction: "If I am going to come to work, I hope I like my job."

3. Motivation to return to work the next day.

Susan M. Heathfield, human resources expert, describes motivation as "an employee's intrinsic enthusiasm and drive to accomplish activities related to work."[19] Someone reading this description might interpret motivation to only come from within a person like a phoenix fire, but a devoted HR professional knows that we are charged with helping light that fire and keeping it burning day after day.

Metaphors like these are the foundation of our workday. We become creative in our efforts to identify a workplace that encourages outside-of-the-box thinkers, dreamers, and innovators. We think the unthinkable and make mere ideas reality in the workplace. They come alive by engraving motivational words on the walls, placing bicycles in the courtyards, building rooms called think tanks, creating human chessboards, buying Nintendo Wiis, strategically setting up Ping-Pong tables in the workspace, and supplying standing workstations to encourage proper ergonomics. While it sounds a bit like an adult toy store or romper room, the purpose is to create a culture of innovative freedom. The return on investment (ROI) is realized when those freaking innovative employee produce creative and forward-looking ideas that will increase profit margin and keep the company one-step ahead of the competition.

Sounds like a love story or a match made in HR heaven to many HR professionals. Make no mistake about it: HR is responsible for speaking the words that motivate winners. You see, behind every great CEO is usually a determined and phenomenal HR executive saying, "Yes, you can!" From time to time there is a brief pause in that go-getter attitude to converse with general counsel to reconfirm our good intentions, but then the enthusiastic CEO along with the HR executive are given the green light to charge forward with swords and shields raised high. Too much? Sorry. The mere thought of motivation takes my excitement into overdrive.

Sometimes motivation starts with a business problem that must be resolved or the need to remain competitive. Other times, motivation starts with the need to be better, do better, and achieve greatness that will be captured in the white papers and history books. Well, that's where HR comes into the creation of the masterpiece. I solemnly believe the adage "Behind every great professional is a GREAT human resources department!" Okay, okay. I know that adage does not exactly read that way. But since I am amongst creative HR professionals, who's to say that it *couldn't* read, "Behind every great man in the workplace is a GREATER HR woman," or vice versa? (This is a gender-friendly book, people.)

Nevertheless, I do believe that HR professionals have been the motivation for many who were recognized for their ingenuity and groundbreaking solutions. These crowning moments of greatness can be likened to a motivation factory because of all the employee lives we have positively changed just by pumping them full of motivation.

I also believe that in moments of despair, when employees think they don't have what it takes to finish the project or, worse yet, don't believe they have what it takes to be great, a kind-hearted HR professional sits down with them and pours a tall, frosty glass of motivation and encourages him or her to not give up.

A not-so-typical day in HR could easily be one with people coming in and out of your office looking for a listening ear because of a recent announcement at a town hall meeting, a rumor at the watercooler, or a recent company press release. But no matter the topic, your door is open, and you are mixing up advice with a shot of encouragement and topping it off with a pep talk.

In between meetings and mixology sessions with employees, you may even be forced to make a trip to the supply room for tissue because the meetings required the drying of tears of sadness, discouragement, or relief. You even sneak a few for yourself in between sessions, as some of the discussions were deeper than you had anticipated, but you held it together and refrained until the coast was clear. If someone asked why your eyes were watering or red, you used the oldie-but-goodie response, "I have something on my contact" or "My allergies are terrible this spring" or "I think I have a cold coming on." You are confident that one of them will work until you remember that you are wearing your glasses, it is winter time, or you just got your flu shot two weeks ago at the health fair in front of God and all your employees. Then you think, Ah, who cares? It is all part of the job—and nobody said you were the Ice Queen or King!

You know that motivation is the key ingredient for returning customers (i.e., employees) and to your overall success in HR. You have cooked with it many times before, and the patrons you call employees have continued to come back for more. You have even gone as far to schedule an in-house training seminar on the topic of motivation for managers, supervisors, and your HR colleagues in need of a refresher. You have been accused of running a motivation factory. While those around you made it sound like a sweatshop, you sent the e-mails and invites anyway, stating that training was mandatory. You forged on, ensuring that the facilitator was prepared and ready to educate your leaders on the importance of motivation, despite the naysayers.

You even scheduled an icebreaker exercise that required each participant to recall a time when someone motivated them to keep up the good work, try harder, never give up, hang in there, failure is not an option, or "we all stumble from time to time but dust ourselves off and try, try again." The testimonies were abundant, as one by one they took a trip down memory lane and remembered that fateful day when motivation took the wheel. They shared numerous stories of triumph over adversity without being called on. At the end, you paused and took a bow, for you had achieved your motivational goal for the session.

YES! The room was oozing with motivation like Nickelodeon green slime, and your soldiers were ready to become motivational gladiators. You felt like Russell Crowe and Olivia Pope combined, but you knew it was all in the name of motivation. You thanked everyone for attending and then turned slowly to exit the room. Suddenly, your imagination took over. The scene was straight out of a movie as your white coat blew in the proverbial wind. Your job there was done.

Bringing yourself back to reality, you know HR professionals have to take each win as it comes because credit where credit is due is limited. To achieve a credit score of 850 is darn near impossible, but you build your credit day by day and try to pay your bills on time. The same holds true in HR: you work hard to build your *credit*ability with employees at all levels within the company because you know someone is cynically keeping score. The trouble with scorecards is that you don't know the high and low score until it is time for 360 reviews, performance reviews, promotions, or salary increases. But being the optimist of the company, you remain hopeful that all you do is more than enough to build and maintain creditability among the troops.

Motivation is free. Share some today.

10

Who, Me?

Did HR Choose You or Did You Choose HR?

Decisions, decisions, decisions. Choices, choices, choices.

Responsibility number one as an HR professional or generalist is to conduct interviews and identify the perfect candidate for vacant or new roles within the company. You are to create a comprehensive job description that prompts qualified candidates to flood the online career portal with résumés and cover letters.

But then one day you realize that the script could or will be flipped. Roles will be reversed, and you will be the job-seeker dusting off and sprucing up your résumé in search of the perfect job. You will be the one who must review the HR job description (which you could have done a much better job creating, but you will never say that out loud since you are the one with no job [real talk]). You must cross-reference your HR skills and job history to a comprehensive job description that someone else wrote. You pause because it makes you feel some-kind-of-way. Focus!

During your review, you have a moment of pause and ask yourself the million- ... scratch that because inflation sucks ... billion-dollar question: Did I choose HR or did HR choose me?

You have a scratch-your-head moment and begin to think, How did I come to this crossroads in my HR career? You then think about the day when you thought long and hard about if you really liked people and could deal with them day in and day out. You think about what it means to be the "go-to HR person" when all hell breaks loose at work. You pause and say in your best "inquiring minds want to know" voice, "Define hell," and your alter ego shares a few scary scenarios that could make this chapter go up in smoke once you're done:

Scenario #1

An employee has been reported by her manager for coming to work intoxicated.

Scenario #2

An employee has been accused of calling another employee an inappropriate name that is not listed on his birth certificate.

Scenario #3

A supervisor touches an employee inappropriately during a closed-door meeting. (Yes, I agree with the voice in your HR head: Why was the freaking door closed anyway?!)

Scenario #4

An employee has a concealed weapon at work and had just received a "needs improvement" on his performance review the day before. (Ah, HELL!)

You cringe just thinking about each scenario and choose to refocus on the question at hand: "Is HR the right career for me?" You shake off the hell-hath-no-fury scenarios and focus instead on the positive scenarios that could set you on the path of HR righteousness:

Scenario #1

You recently made the decision to obtain a business degree with a concentration in HR.

Scenario #2

You reconsider the degree and accept an internship or HR assistant job to explore the inner workings of the *glamorous* life of HR.

Scenario #3

You remember friends or family members who have chosen HR as a career and the stories they shared (minus the confidential information, of course). You recall how each one concluded with how they helped others in need navigate the good and bad times. You remember how that made you feel all warm and fuzzy inside (not the gremlin-in-the-daytime-before-you-feed-them fuzzy, but a "I volunteered at a homeless shelter on Christmas Day" fuzzy).

And suddenly, just like that, you realize that you *chose* HR as your career!

Moment of Truth: So my career in HR did not follow the path of least resistance and therefore *did not choose HR*. I vividly recall the day when I just needed a job to inject some income into my household so me and my family could eat and keep a roof over our heads. I remember the day when a local employer posted an ad for a receptionist position in the local newspaper (before Indeed.com, folks) at a small company that specialized in an industry that was of no particular interest to me except that they had a freaking job opening. The job description stated the company was seeking a qualified candidate who was a fast learner with basic computer and organization skills and had a friendly and courageous demeanor. The ad stated that résumés should be sent to a local address not far from my home, and I thought to myself, I am that person!

Then reality hit when I remembered I didn't even have a résumé. I prayed they would forgive my ignorance and had an application I could complete because I had been keeping my job history in a notebook from my old high school days. Lord, help me! But despite not having a résumé, I was confident and prepared for a challenge. No one could dim my flame and tell me that I freaking couldn't do the job.

So I located the mailing address and decided I would pay the company a visit instead. There is something to be said for blind ambition, but I was young and ambitious and just needed glasses.

I marched in the door dressed in my best job-search, come-hither suit and was greeted by the HR manager. I conveyed my interest, and—*voilà!*—I was invited to stay for an interview. I found out during the walk to the interview room that the HR manager would be interviewing me because not only was she the HR manager, she was also the person the receptionist would report to. I remember taking a deep breath and saying to myself, "No pressure, right?" But I knew the pressure was on and my best game face was required if I was to be the "soup of the day and asked to stay" (in my best jingle voice).

About fifteen minutes into the interview, I realized that it absolutely made freaking sense that the receptionist reported to the HR department because both roles required that the person be a people person, polite, courteous, and a fast learner. My personality radiated like a diamond during the interview, and I was complimented on my smile and sense of humor. (Who knew I would write a book about HR and having a sense of humor twenty-five years later?)

Two days later, I received a call from the HR manager who extended what HR professionals call a verbal offer of employment, and I accepted without hesitation. (Obviously, I was still an amateur and knew nothing about negotiation and counteroffers, but I would learned in due time.)

Then six months later, I was in awe of the role that my boss, the HR manager, played in the company. I watched her treat my colleagues like customers, serve their needs with a smile, and offer empathy when necessary. I admired her problem-solving skills and how fast she thought on her feet when a crisis occurred in the workplace. I respected her more and more every day for maintaining confidentiality when requested and required. I realized that nothing really got done without her blessing, even though the president of the company thought he was in charge. I worked hard every day, watching and taking mental notes of her actions and the reaction of staff each time she gave an order, guidance, or feedback.

Then my day came when I was a customer of hers and she applied those freaking amazing HR techniques and tactics as she worked to resolve my issue. Her compassion and swift reaction to my needs still leave me speechless and emotional twenty-five years later. In that moment, I knew that the role she held was what I wanted to be when I grew up. It was then that *HR chose me* for the first but certainly not the last time. On that day, I decided that I wanted to be a "resource to humans" in need. I also would later coin the following edict that I would share with my future employees: "Employees are not just social security numbers and names on a list. They are real people, just like you, who need our help to demystify the world we call HR."

Fast-Forward: So I end this chapter as I started it. HR professionals, near and far, ask yourselves, "Did HR choose you, or did you choose HR?" No matter your answer, say it with your shoulders back and head held high! Also, remember to remain steadfast and confident that no matter the journey that led you to become an HR professional, you are a valuable member of the company you serve and worth your weight in ... EMPLOYEE HANDBOOKS!

Open your own door, walk through it,
and never look back.

11

The Climb, the Descent, and the Reinvent

Career. That single word continues to evolve in meaning and has varying levels of credibility and periods of longevity. When someone says the word "career," it encompasses all jobs (including HR), and therefore the climb, the descent, and the need to reinvent oneself applies to all who will listen.

HR professionals, and others like us, are proud to share that they have risen to notoriety during their careers. They chose their career paths carefully, certain to connect and build relationships with the right people in high places, gaining visibility wherever possible, such as company meetings, town halls, family picnics, and after-hours social gatherings. Visibility was, and still is, the name of the game.

The Climb

Taking the metaphoric elevator to the top of the job scale makes perfect sense and shows progressiveness in one's career. Innocent but intentional thoughts of replacing the person in the role of your heart's desire dance like sugar plums through your head, and it isn't even Christmas. Then suddenly, you are a rising star, climbing the mountain of success.

You wake up one day and find you have a calendar invite to meet with the CEO (AKA mob boss) to accept an assignment from the Godfather or Godmother (must ensure equality, even at the top). You dare not say, "No" or "Let me think about it" for fear it will be viewed as a sign of weakness and ingratitude by those in high places. So you graciously accept the position without hesitation, even though you know that another person is still technically in the role. You think to yourself, Oh well. Not my problem. I'll let HR handle the details while I bask in the afterglow of my success. You then pause and say to yourself, "Heck, HR should have been called first when they were outlining my transition plan!"

Certainly that is correct. But let's step outside the afterglow for a moment and take refuge in the reality that the CEO most likely made the decision and went so far as to share the promotion news with the employee before consulting HR. Because he was so freaking excited, or maybe because of the little thing we call ego, he wanted to be the first to publicly share. Who will ever know the real reason? It is done!

Post-cat out of the bag, HR receives the call and in comes the cleanup crew. The company organizational charts are printed, performance reviews are pulled, succession plans and the nine-box diagram are dusted off, and in a shake of a not-so-typical day in HR, a plan is presented and your promotion to the new position is announced via company e-mail and good ol' word of mouth. Thanks, HR, for coming to the rescue—again.

After serving a few good years in your new role, your career switches to cruise control. Life is good! The position of your dreams is all that and a bag of sweet potato chips, and the view from the top is spectacular.

The Descent

Then one day the company announces a merger with a competitor company that will result in a change in leadership because Mr. High Places decided he would voluntarily retire (we have heard that one before) to seek more life balance and less work balance. Give me a freaking break. There goes the neighborhood when even the popular term "work/life balance" is diluted by the people on high. Darn if HR hasn't been using this as a mantra to promote goodwill among the troops, and now look what they have gone and done—used it to vacate a position because of duplication of roles at the top! Ever heard of two CEOs? Nope, me neither. So hang on, as the descent is about to begin—just like that.

Without any notice, the new CEO calls an audible from his playbook, which includes strategically replacing all senior management reporting to him. The Os depict his team and the Xs, which include you, the old team. Three words: this freaking sucks! Your focus then turns from *doing* your job to *saving* your job, which is a sad state of affairs that may end in a hideous performance review. Nevertheless, you are only human, so your attention turns to yourself because it is every man or woman for him- or herself in this cutthroat business. You begin writing a long list of your accomplishments because you feel you have served honorably in this role and must share pronto with the new leadership team if you are to survive.

Moment of Truth: I have experienced the climb in my career because of my mentors, for whom I am forever grateful. The climb was definitely all that and a bag of sweet potato chips. I strived to remain humble during those times because I strongly believe that humility and tact are a part of the HR creed. I graciously accepted each promotion, knowing that they don't come without hard work and perseverance. Yes, working with people during their most sensitive times has made me empathetic and appreciative of even less than 10 percent grade climbs. I have been fortunate to not experience the involuntary descent in my career, but I respect it nonetheless. It only takes being the bearer of demotion (descent) news to employees to understand the sting of defeat and humiliation. While the climb builds confidence in rising stars, the descent crushes confidence and self-esteem. This is when HR professionals must be the voice of understanding and empathy.

Fast-Forward: You are offered a demotion or a severance package because another rising star has been selected by senior management to fill your position. You struggle to find the words. You were once that rising star, and you recall how you thought only for a very brief moment about your predecessor during your climb to the top. But you don't sulk too much because you remember the "Purple Rain" and must exercise some humility and roll with the fruit punches, even though it is not 100 percent juice. You accept the severance package because although you are humble, your pride still has been hurt and you don't want to stick around for the nose-rubbing and lame descent-and-demotion apologies.

Reinvent

This is the moment you realize you were in your dream job for more than a few years. Darn how time flies when you are in the climb! The calendar says it was more like five years, and the job market has changed and moved on without you. You freak out, feeling like the employee time has forgotten and shout, "What do I freaking do now?" It feels like you are waiting at the train station but the train never comes and the market no longer finds you sexy.

You gather yourself after your Sahara Desert meltdown and remember your wonderful HR director during your exit interview sharing information regarding career transition and outplacement services that are offered to severed employees. You shuffle through your large termination package after taking a quick look again at your severance agreement and say, "Six weeks. I better get my life together or be left eating ramen noodles." You find the details about one of the most prestigious outplacement companies in the region. The package offers leadership coaching, assistance with revamping your résumé, access to their proprietary job boards, and key networking opportunities. The offer is like peanut butter to your jelly now that you have a scarlet *R* for "reject" painted on your business suit. You immediately make the call to begin your personal consultation.

You review your overall skills with your peer-level coach and are advised it is time to … wait for it … reinvent yourself if you expect to jump on the next train when it arrives at the station. Reinvent? Does this mean you now must request a patent for some new hamburger-patty grill as your next career? You gather yourself and exit the emotion and pride zone, understanding what you are being ask to do and recognizing that you are more than your prior role and cannot let that define or lame-duck you. You realize that you only have to scratch your ass(ets) a bit. And there, right below the surface of your old four-page résumé are the notable skills and experiences that will be highlighted in your reinvigorated résumé and marketing plan.

In that moment, you sing a few bars of Donna Summer's "I Will Survive."

Potential is within and just waiting for your invitation to take the runway.

12

Sue Me, Please!

Attention, HR professionals! This chapter is a not a public service announcement or an invitation to employees to sue their employers. This is a reminder to you that employees can, and will, sue if you are not familiar with general employment legislation. It is also highly recommended that your company or firm partner with a trustworthy general counsel specializing in employment law. While this topic is serious, I recommend that you have a sense of humor when on the HR battlefield because you will have some conversations that will appear to be common sense in context but somehow the other person or persons will miss the punch line. It is your duty to be ready for the conversation and to help with aha moments.

In 2014, the US Equal Employment Opportunity Commission (EEOC) reported that 88,778 individual charges were filed and resolved under all statutes enforced by the EEOC (Title VII, Americans with Disability Act, Age Discrimination and Employment Act, Environmental Protection Agency, and Genetic Information Nondiscrimination Act). Total monetary price tag: $296.1 million, which was down from $372.1 million in 2013.[20] While 65 percent of the claims were dropped, the fact is we can't make this stuff up. Being armed with a few basic facts and reminders can help tremendously and aid HR in sounding the fire alarm when someone is about to go through the valley of the shadow of death because they have experienced, or are, evil.

In this chapter, I will outline a few employment law reminders that can be applied quickly and potentially discourage an employee from taking me up on my humorous invitation. I will also slip-and-slide in the following legal disclaimer for your reading pleasure and my legal protection:

I have made every effort to offer ethical, accurate, and commonsense HR workplace advice in this book. I am not an attorney (not even on TV). The content in this chapter is not guaranteed for legality and is not to be construed as legal advice.

Executive Decision Making

According to a study conducted by Columbia University, CEOs take only *nine minutes* to make 50 percent of company decisions.[21] Therefore, it is important that we ask our CEOs and decision makers to slow down when making decisions. We should encourage them to test their thinking—think *60 Minutes, TMZ,* or *CNN*—and then see if they would like to increase the time to at least thirty minutes. HR and legal counsel should join forces and point out a few additional local, regional, and national news agencies that would be happy to quickly spread bad news about the company. Perhaps this, too, will slow the process a bit. We need to remind our CEOs that their decisions set the precedent for future activity that HR will have to consider when attempting to defuse future incidents. In doing so, my hope is that they will call for a time-out and remember to consult with the new team called Regal (HR and Legal—get it?).

Finally, always remember that HR's role is to be a resource to the CEO, not to say yes or no, but to advise how to manage and avoid, or at least reduce, risk. Leave the courtroom drama for Judge Judy.

Hiring and Firing

During the recruiting process, is HR interviewing the candidate or is the candidate interviewing the company? The answer is *"Both."* If the goal is to recruit the A-list candidates, companies must ask, "Why would an A-list player want to work for us?" and be prepared to respond with a Specific, Measurable, Achievable, Relevant, Timely (SMART) answer.

HR and management should think about how the company's résumé looks while rehearsing this answer. For instance, does the company have a long list of EEOC and unemployment claims on record? When the potential candidate uses his or her favorite Internet browser, will dirt about the company appear at the top of the list? Any history of these types of infractions may not appeal to an A-list candidate seeking to shelter from the storm. Company image is everything, and taking several looks in the mirror is always a good idea to ensure their proverbial mascara is not smudged and toupee is not out of place.

On the flip side, HR and hiring managers should think about firing before hiring. Yes, you read that correctly. If the company understands the risk and the cost necessary to fix an employment relationship gone bad, then they are less likely to make the same mistake in the future. This tactic will also require HR to take its own advice and *slow down*. You see, firing is a strategy.

When asked the following two questions, do you conclude that the company's hiring process was key to mitigating involuntary terminations?

1. Are you proud of the employees who work for you?

2. Would you rehire your direct reports?

The rule of thumb is to be methodical in your hiring process, which can decease your company's firing statistics.

However, when firing is necessary, and the company knows the employee is going to sue, do it immediately. Don't wait. Don't be held hostage by the employee and asked to pay ransom in the form of performance improvement plans (PIP) that delay the inevitable and allow the employee to wreak havoc in the workplace for thirty, sixty, or ninety days.

But it is important that you understand the written policies and commitment made in an offer letter if you are considering firing an employee. Does your company have a ninety-day probationary period? Why? Word of advice: if the probationary period is not required by a union or state mandate, don't put it in writing. Why? An employee can have poor performance for eighty-eight days and then on day eighty-nine call HR and his manager and say, "Help me." Freaking *great*! Putting probationary language in writing in an employee handbook or policy will make it contractual, and the company may be faced with implementing a sound PIP policy or firing the employee and awaiting the lawsuit. The odds will most likely not be in the company's favor, even if you won twenty dollars on a two-dollar scratch ticket last week. It will be hammer time, and the company will need to saddle up and be prepared to defend itself against charges that the dismissal was illegal.

Next rule of thumb: document, document, document! Documentation is the name of this game, and Regal must provide legitimate reasons for the termination, including examples of poor performance, supervisor and review notes, and verbal and written warnings to the terminated employee. Also, remember that all documentation is discoverable, so be ready to open the electronic and desk drawers.

Written Policies

Inventory time. What written policies do you have in place at your company? Severance policy? Myth buster: employers are not required to offer severance packages to terminated employees, with the exception of state mandates and large reduction in force. However, paying severance as an act of goodwill to long-tenured employees for their service may make sense and be good publicity for the company. Remember those A-listers you may need to hire in the future? But if your company's severance policy is in writing, be prepared to pay severance to the masses because you made a promise most likely in an employee handbook or book of personnel policies that outlines how much severance the company will pay an employee if he or she is terminated).[22] There will be no take-backs, and HR should be prepared to review and customize those lengthy boilerplate template agreements.

Bereavement policy? Bad things do happen to good people, and HR is the first in line to strongly encourage managers to support employees when they need time off to mourn and make arrangements for the loss of a loved one. Gut-check questions:

1. How does HR verify bereavement?

    a. Take a photo? (No pictures, please!)

    b. Request a copy of the death certificate? (What file are you going to keep this in? Benefits? Employment?)

2. Who does the bereavement policy cover?

    a. Immediate family? (Not that language again! Whose to say that his or her second cousin wasn't like a sister or brother?)

The solution to this HR administrative madness could be as simple as folding the bereavement policy into the company paid time off (PTO) policy. Aha moment, right? Yep! While this might result in the increase of PTO days as a whole, it will go a long way in garnering cool points and this definitely make a fabulous submission for "Best Place to Work."

Below are a few more policies and best-practice quick tips laced with a sense of humor for you out-of-box HR professionals to consider:

- Avoid dating policy. Company can't really prove through nightly bed check, so try to avoid.

- Consider updating the dress code policy if there are any references to "two inches above or below the knee." Consider hosting a dress-for-success employee meeting with a visual-aid presentation. It is hard to find wooden rulers or tape measures in the office these days anyway.

- If you are conducting an exit interview for an employee who quit, why are you asking, "Why did you quit?" It's too late! As an alternative, consider calling him or her in six weeks rather than talking to him or her on the last day of employment. The smoke has then had time to clear, and you will not need security!

- Got a great on-boarding practice? Do you talk to employees, especially the Millennials, at the end of the first day? You should! As the word on the street has it, employees start looking for work at the end of the first day if they don't find the job all they dreamed it would be. Sorry to burst bubbles, but this is a quick fix for great HR professionals with open minds.

- Say it with me, "Up to and including termination of employment." Freaking remove it, and don't say it again in your disciplinary communication (e.g., handbooks, warning letters, performance reviews, etc.). Replace it with a general or behavioral statement that has been approved by legal counsel. "Say what you mean and mean what you say" is the name of this game.[23]

Start smart and finish smarter.

13

HR Acronyms and Lingo: What Did You Just Say?

Can you remember your first official day in HR? If you are among the choice few who took your ginseng or have been completing those Sudoku puzzles, then you probably can. But if not, no harm or foul because this chapter is to simply remind you of all the acronyms and lingo spoken during a typical and not-so-typical day in HR.

Moment of Truth: I remember thinking during my first day, Is anyone going to tell me what that acronym and word freaking means? Unfortunately, nobody did, so I just jotted down the letters (or how I thought the acronym or word sounded) and told myself that I would look it up later or ask someone who looked like he or she would not give me the stink eye when I confessed to not knowing what the heck they were talking about during the meeting. I even remember laughing and saying, "Did she just say that Gladys Knight and the "Pips" were in trouble and we handled their HR issues too?"

Fast-Forward: So in the spirit of sharing and to help others so they don't find themselves in the same situation, to follow are a few acronyms that can be helpful to entry-level HR professionals and a refresher to experienced HR gurus. The list is also a stark reminder of how we have gone freaking crazy with acronyms because we have run out of time to say the entire phrase.

- AAP—Affirmative Action Plan

- AAR—After Action Review

- ACA—Affordable Care Act

- ADEA—Age Discrimination in Employment Act

- AE—Annual Enrollment

- AR—Annual Review

- BEER—Behavior, Effect, Expectation, Results (for feedback for improvement)

- BET—Behavior, Effect, Thanks (for positive feedback)

- CAUSED—**Can** they do it? Do they have a positive **Attitude**? Is it **Useful** to them? Are they **Skilled** in it? Do they have similar **Experience**? Is it **Different**?

- DUMBER—Dull, Unrealistic, Mediocre, Boring, Evaporating, Rote

- EAP—Employee Assistance Program

- EEOC—Equal Employment Opportunity Commission

- EI—Employee Involvement

- EPA—Equal Pay Act

- FLSA—Fair Labor Standards Act

- FMLA—Family Medical Leave Act

- FSA—Flexible Spending Account

- HR—Human Resources

- HSA—Health Savings Account

- HS&E—Health, Safety, and Environmental

- IDEAL—**Identify** the problem, **Define** and represent the problem, **Explore** possible strategies, **Act** on the strategies, **Look** back and evaluate the effects of your actions

- IP—Interpersonal

- IRCA—Immigration Reform and Control Act

- IRS—Internal Revenue Service

- KISS—Keep It Simple, Stupid

- L&D—Learning and Development

- LMS—Learning Management System

- LOA—Leave of Absence

- LTD—Long-Term Disability

- MOP—Measure of Performance

- NEO—New Employee Orientation

- NLRB—National Labor Relations Board

- OD—Organization Development

- OE—Open Enrollment (for health benefits)

- OSHA—Occupational Safety and Health Administration

- PA—Performance Assessment

- PIP—Performance Improvement Plan

- PPM—Policy and Procedures Manual

- PR—Performance Review

- QA—Quality Assurance

- SMART—Specific, Measurable, Achievable, Relevant, Timely

- SMARTER—Specific, Measurable, Achievable, Relevant, Timely, Exciting, Recorded

- SOP—Standard Operating Procedure

- TBNT—Thanks But No Thanks

- WC—Workers' Compensation

Did you know that HR lingo can be just as comical as HR acronyms? Just when you thought your degree and on-the-job experience was enough in the early stages of your career, you found out that words in HR don't quite translate to the standard definition. So much for being "SMART but finding out that it really means "specific, measurable, achievable, relevant, and timely" in HR lingo.

The following list of HR glossary terms was developed by the SHRM Knowledge Center and is not all-inclusive of HR and general business terminology, but rather includes terms in daily use by HR professionals.[24] I have added my humorous translations because, you will admit that you were thinking these things anyway!

Terms	Definition	Humorous Translation
Adverse impact	A substantially different rate of selection in hiring, promotion or other employment decision that works to the disadvantage of a race, sex or ethnic group.	A no-no!
Bell-curve	The curve representing the normal distribution of a rating or test score.	At what point in the bell-curve should we panic?
Climate survey	A tool used to solicit and assess employee opinions, feelings, perceptions and expectations regarding a variety of factors pertinent to maintaining the organization climate.	In case they hate us, point me to the emergency exit first!

Terms	Definition	Humorous Translation
Decentralization	The process of assigning decision-making authority to lower levels within the organization hierarchy.	Mark your calendar for the centralization party because they always come back!
Emotional intelligence	Describing the mental ability an individual possesses enabling him or her to be sensitive and understanding to the emotions of others, as well as to manage his or her own emotions and impulses.	What? There are others even more emotional than HR?
Flat organization	An organization characterized by having only a few layers of management from top to bottom.	Perfect number of chiefs and Indians.

Terms	Definition	Humorous Translation
Glass ceiling	Used to describe the invisible barriers keeping women from advancing into executive-level positions.	Watch for broken glass because times are changing!
Halo effect	A form of interviewer bias, occurring when the interviewer rates or judges an individual based on the individual's positive or strongest traits, allowing their overall perception of the person to overshadow any negative traits.	I want mine in a size eight and in white with glitter, please.

Terms	Definition	Humorous Translation
Icebreaker	A beginning exercise, game or simulation used as a means to reduce tension and create a more relaxed atmosphere during training programs.	Will there be a psychiatrist and a couch for this exercise?
Job bank	Refers to pools of retired employees who are used by employers to fill part-time or temporary position needs.	I'd like to make a withdrawal!
Key performance indicators (KPI)	Quantifiable, specific measures of an organization's performance in a certain area(s) of the business.	So are you saying that being good is not enough information?

Terms	Definition	Humorous Translation
Lockout/tagout rule	An OSHA standard helping safeguard employees from hazardous energy while they are performing services or maintenance on machines and equipment.	Is that why my badge didn't work?
Matrix organization	An organization structure where employees report to more than one manager or supervisor.	As if one supervisor is not enough!
Nepotism	Favoritism shown to relative by individuals in a position of authority, such as managers or supervisors.	Didn't you hear that Queen Nefertiti and King Tut are in the same tomb?

Terms	Definition	Humorous Translation
Outsourcing	A contractual agreement between an employer and an external third-party provider whereby the employer transfers responsibility and management for certain HR, benefits, or training-related functions or services to the external provider.	Did you say you are paying someone to have an affair with another company?
Perquisites	A form of incentives generally given to executive employees granting them certain privileges or special consideration.	And just like that, the word "perks" was born. Who knew?

Terms	Definition	Humorous Translation
Quid pro quo	Legal terminology essentially meaning "what for what" or "something for something". It is the concept of getting something of value in exchange for giving something of value.	Look, Hannibal Lecter, that is between you and Clarice. So leave me out of it!
Retention bonus	An incentive payment used to entice employees from leaving organization after signing an agreement stating they will remain employed for a specific duration or completion of a task or project in order to be eligible for bonus.	You had me at hello ... I mean, bonus!
Salting	Refers to paid union organizers who apply for jobs with an employer for the purpose of organizing the employer's workforce.	Talk about throwing salt in the game! So if that is salting, when do we get to use the pepper spray?

Terms	Definition	Humorous Translation
Think tank	A group organized for the purpose of intensive research and problem solving, especially in the area of technology, social or political strategy, or demographics.	Don't forget to bring your swimsuit and goggles.
Upward mobility	The process of preparing minorities for promotion into higher-level jobs, such as managerial positions.	Before we get started, is there such a thing as downward mobility?
Virtual HR	The use of technology to provide HR programs via an employee self-service platform. Typically includes use of such items as voice response systems, employee kiosks, etc.	You mean HR can now officially work from home? Grab your coffee cup.

Terms	Definition	Humorous Translation
Work/life balance	Having a measure of control over when, where and how an individual works, so individual is able to enjoy an optimal quality of life.	How's that working for you?
Zero-based budgeting	A budgeting system that starts with no authorized funds as a starting point. In zero-based budget, each activity or program to be funded must be justified every time a new budget is prepared and resources are allocated accordingly.	I knew they wanted me to work for free when they made me that lame offer!

Words shape perception.
Perception shapes reality.

14

My Favorite HR Resources

In the wonderful world of HR, I rely on information that will make my job easier. While I would love to say I can retain all the best HR practices, legislation, and rules to live by, I can't. So I am sharing a list of some of my favorite HR resources. If you are a rising star in HR, I hope you find this helpful in your climb to the top. If you are an experienced HR guru, we are in the boat together. Please browse, and give yourself a high five!

- United States Department of Labor www.dol.gov

- US Equal Employment Opportunity Commission www.eeoc.gov

- World Federation of People Management Associations (WFPMA) www.wfpma.com

- North American Human Resource Management Association (NAHRMA) www.nahrma.com

- Society for Human Resource Management (SHRM) www.shrm.org

- HR Certification Institute www.hrci.org

- HR Houston www.hrhouston.org

- National Association of African-Americans in Human Resources www.naaahr.org

- HR.com www.hr.com

- International Foundation of Employee Benefit Plans www.ifebp.org

- American Benefits Council www.americanbenefitscouncil.org

- Salary.com www.salary.com

- Talent Management and HR (TLNT) www.tlnt.com

- HR.BLR.com www.hr.blr.com

- Human Resource Management Review www.journals.elsevier.com/human-resource-management-review/

- HR Morning www.hrmorning.com

- Kaiser Family Foundation www.kff.org

- Legal Zoom www.legalzoom.com

- Lee Hecht Harrison www.lhh.com

- *USA Today* www.usatoday.com

- *Wall Street Journal* www.wsj.com

- Dun & Bradstreet www.dandb.com

Learning from others is a gift, not a crime.

About the Author

Carol McBride is the author of *HR, Where's Your Freaking Sense of Humor* and so glad you choose to read and learn more about her freaking sense of humor! Carol is also the Founder and Managing Partner of The Carol McBride Group, LLC (CMG).

Carol grew up in the historic Park Hill community of Denver, Colorado. She attended primary and secondary schools in the neighboring communities and graduated from George Washington High School a semester ahead of her 1988 class because of her freaking determination. She was a teen-mother when she had her beautiful and extraordinary daughter, Ashley, and quickly developed survival skills as a single mom. She was freaking determined to discredit the teen-mother stereotype that statistically prophesized that she would succumb to poverty and dependence on social services.

She later had her handsome and brilliant son, Jonathon, and the three of them became dependent on one another until 2008 when she married the man of her dreams, Bobby McBride. Together, they have continued to build a life focused on God, family, and having a freaking sense of humor. She and her husband now live in suburbs of Houston, Texas. Her daughter is now happily married and lives in the Houston area and her son, also has left the nest and lives in Houston.

She holds a Bachelor of Science in Business degree with a concentration in human resources and has worked as a HR professional for more than 20 years. She is also a Certified Professional in Human Resources (PHR) specializing in Global Health and Welfare, Retirement, and Pension. She currently is Senior Consultant at one of the top human capital consulting firms in the U.S. During her 20-year tenure in HR, she has demonstrated her ability to exceed entrepreneur and corporate objectives in a variety of senior HR management and entrepreneurial roles.

She is known for her ability to generate successful HR outcomes in industries ranging from healthcare to environmental science to technology to oil and gas services. She has an impressive reputation for being a strategic change agent, inspiring facilitator, and motivational speaker. She has been praised for her innate ability to understand complex HR topics and translate content into laymen's terms for audiences of all types.

She has made numerous public speaking and personal appearances at various notable events in Denver, Colorado and Houston, Texas. She also appeared on the American quiz show "You Bet Your Life," and was a special guest on the "Jenny Jones" show where she was recognized for her accomplishments as Miss Black Colorado, USA.

Notes

[1] *Merriam-Webster*, s.v. "mantra," accessed July 1, 2015, http://www.merriam-webster.com/dictionary/personnel.

[2] "Quotes About Mentoring," Goodreads, Inc., accessed September 1, 2015, http://www.goodreads.com,/quotes/tag/mentoring?page=4.

[3] "Quotes About Inspired Thoughts," Goodreads, Inc., accessed September 1, 2015, http://www.goodreads.com/quotes/tag/inspired-thoughts.

[4] "Reverse Mentoring Cracks Workplace," Leslie Kwoh, *The Wall Street Journal*, November 28, 2011, accessed July 1, 2015, http://www.wsj.com/articles/SB10001424052970203764804577 060051461094004.

[5] "The Advantages of Mentoring in the Workplace," Janice Tingum, Demand Media, *Houston Chronicle*, accessed September 1, 2015, http://smallbusiness.chron.com/advantages-mentoring-workplace-18437.html.

[6] Mississippi Sheiks & Chatman Brothers, *"Old Grey Mule, You Ain't What You Used To Be,"* 1934–1936, Document Records, DOCD-5086, Record.

[7] "Baby Boomer Generation Fast Facts," CNN, August 24, 2015, accessed September 1, 2015, http://www.cnn.com/2013/11/06/us/baby-boomer-generation-fast-facts/.

[8] "Baby Boomers," History.com Staff, History.com, 2010, http://www.history.com/topics/baby-boomers.

[9] "What Age Group Makes Up Generation X (Gen X)?," Susan M. Heathfield, About.com, accessed September 1, 2015, http://humanresources.about.com/od/glossaryg/g/gen_x.htm.

[10] "15 Economic Facts About Millennials," The Council of Economic Advisers, October 2014, accessed September 1, 2015, https://www.whitehouse.gov/administration/eop/cea/factsheets-reports.

11 "Offices vs. Cubicles: What's the Better Workplace Environment?" Glassdoor Team, Glassdoor Blog, August 19, 2009, accessed September 15, 2015, http://www.glassdoor.com/blog/offices-cubicles-whats-workplace-environment/.

12 "The 3 Stages of Organizational Development," Dr. Roger K. Allen, The Center for Organizational Design, February 2012, accessed October 15, 2015, http://www.centerod.com/2012/02/3-stages-organizational-development/.

13 *Merriam-Webster*, s.v. "personnel," accessed July 1, 2015, http://www.merriam-webster.com/dictionary/personnel.

14 "The Evolution of HR: Developing HR as an Internal Consulting Organization," Richard M. Vosburgh, Human Resources Planning 30.3, August 31, 2015, accessed September 25, 2015, http://c.ymcdn.com/sites/www.hrps.org/resource/resmgr/p_s_article_preview/hrps_issue30.3_evolutionofhr.pdf.

15 "The Practical Guide to Mergers, Acquisitions, and Divestitures," Delta Publishing Company, accessed August 27, 2015, http://www.apexcpe.com/publications/171025.pdf.

16 "Rumors in the Workplace," People Communicating, accessed August 14, 2015, http://www.people-communicating.com/rumors-in-the-workplace.html.

17 "There Are Significant Business Costs to Replacing Employees," Heather Boushey and Sarah Jane Glynn, accessed October 6, 2015, https://www.americanprogress.org/issues/labor/report/2012/11/16/44464/there-are-significant-business-costs-to-replacing-employees/.

18 "5 Ways to Manage Turnover," Eric Krell, accessed October 7, 2015, http://www.shrm.org/publications/hrmagazine/editorialcontent/2012/0412/pages/0412krell.aspx#sthash.W2JZjhIf.dpuf.

19 "What Is Employee Motivation?," Dr. Susan M. Heathfield, About.com, accessed August 15, 2015, http://humanresources.about.com/od/glossarye/g/employee-motivation.htm.

[20] "All Statutes FY 1997–FY 2014," U.S. Equal Employment Opportunity Commission, accessed July 17, 2015, http://www.eeoc.gov/eeoc/statistics/enforcement/all.cfm.

[21] "How to make choosing easier," Sheena Iyengar, Ted Conference, LLC, accessed August 10, 2015, http://www.ted.com/talks/sheena_iyengar_choosing_what_to_c hoose/transcript?language=en#t-30000.

[22] "Severance Pay Laws: Does It Make Sense to Offer Severance Pay?," FindLaw, accessed June 12, 2015, http://smallbusiness.findlaw.com/employment-law-and-human-resources/severance-pay-laws-does-it-make-sense-to-offer-severance-pay.html.

[23] Special thanks to Hunter Lott for approving the use of this information. Visit his website at www.hunterlott.com.

[24] "Originally published as Glossary of Human Resources Terms," SHRM Knowledge Center, © 2004, Society for Human Resource Management, Alexandria, VA. Used with permission. All rights reserved, accessed October 8, 2015, http://www.shrm.org/TemplatesTools/Glossaries/Documents/G LOSSARY%20OF%20HUMAN%20RESOURCES%20TERM S.pdf.

Printed in Great Britain
by Amazon